Understanding Copyright

Copyright

————— A Practical Guide —————

Eric A Thorn

Jay books

Jay books
30 The Boundary, Langton Green, Tunbridge Wells, Kent TN3 0YB, England

Other titles by Eric A. Thorn include:

A Question of Copyright (Jay books)
Let's Sing and Make Music (Jay books)
Project the Right Image (Jay books)
The Chosen Few (with Roger Jones) (Christian Music Ministries)
Tell Me the Stories of Jesus (with Roger Jones) (McCrimmon)

First published 1989
© Eric A. Thorn 1989

British Library Cataloguing in Publication Data

Thorn, Eric A. (Eric Arnold), *1948–*
    Understanding copyright: a practical guide.
    1. Great Britain. Copyright. Law
    I. Title
    344.1064'82

    ISBN 1-870404-03-3

Cartoons by Robert Sayell
Cover design by Jenny Clouter
Photoset by MC Typeset Ltd, Gillingham, Kent
Printed by The Whitefriars Press Ltd, Tonbridge, Kent

Contents

Disclaimer

Because of its complexities, copyright legislation has been found open to many and varied interpretations. The comments in this book are based on the author's personal view of the copyright laws in the United Kingdom.

Neither the author nor the publishers can accept any liability for any matters arising from the opinions and conclusions conveyed in this publication, which are offered for guidance only.

If you, or any organization you are involved with, have particular problems concerning copyright, you are advised to obtain professional advice from a solicitor dealing with copyright matters.

Acknowledgements

The author and publishers would like to thank the many people and organizations who have so freely assisted in the preparation of this book. Questions have been answered. Corrections have been made. Permission to use illustrations and quotations has been granted. If any item has not been duly credited we apologize. Please advise the publishers so that this may be corrected in any future edition.

Foreword _____

Copyright is not some remote concept; it touches everyone of us constantly as we go about our daily business or find relaxation in leisure pursuits, for copyright is involved with practically everything we read, look at or listen to. It subsists in books, newspapers, journals, magazines, music, maps, illustrations, paintings, photographs, discs and videos, motion pictures, television and radio broadcasts, theatrical productions and much more recently computer programs and databases. We live in an information driven society that demands access to both knowledge and entertainment, and copyright encourages the creation and dissemination of original works of authorship at prices people can afford. As thinkers, writers and artists meet the needs of the modern world so copyright provides a system by which society can reward these creators.

Almost inevitably copyright has become a highly specialized subject, made more complex in recent years because of the technology that has revolutionized human communications. The photocopier has superseded the duplicator; plastic and paper printing plates now frequently replace metal typesetting; desk top publishing and laser printing are becoming widely accessible; fax machines are taking over from telex; computer capabilities widen all the time; the storage capacity of CD-ROM is astounding, while optical scanners transfer text from one format to another with awe-inspiring speed and facility.

For most people copyright is a confusing subject; there is a lamentable lack of understanding of what copyright is, what it does and why it is so important. There is a clear need for an uncomplicated guide to copyright, and this book meets it admirably. Written in plain English, it unravels the legal complexities and in concise fashion explains the concepts and the law and then tells how the institution and the individual can comply with their copyright obligations.

Eric A. Thorn has been involved with the publishing and printing industries for a number of years and his earlier booklets *Caution – Copyright* and *A Question of Copyright* were widely referred to and rightly admired. This book has been written to take account of the changes in copyright law that have come about with the passing of the Copyright, Designs and Patents Act 1988 that has now replaced the Copyright Act 1956. It is a sobering thought that there is now unlikely to be any major revision of UK copyright law until after the year 2020! This book, I am sure, will have run to many editions before then.

Colin P. Hadley

Introduction

Intellectual works should be encouraged and shared. This belief has been held strongly for hundreds of years.

Such works can be categorized under many and various headings: literature, music, art, audio and video recordings, computer programs, radio and television broadcasts and facsimile (fax) transmissions – to name some of the more familiar. The common denominator of all these works of human intellect is that they each attract one or more rights in reproduction processes; in other words – *copyrights*. These works are now commonly referred to as *intellectual property*, and its interesting to note that a White Paper outlining proposals for new copyright legislation, prepared by the Department of Trade and Industry and issued by Her Majesty's Government in April 1986, was given the title *Intellectual Property and Innovation*.

Intellectual property differs dramatically from other forms of property in two ways. Firstly, it is abstract. Secondly, once it has been produced in a tangible format, it is extremely vulnerable to easy exploitation, particularly since the development of modern reproductive technology. It is temptingly easy to photocopy magazine articles or sheet music at the local library.

Other 'non-intellectual' types of property, by contrast, require investment and possibly special skills for their reproduction. The livelihood of bakers is not at risk from a nation of 'do-it-yourself' breadmakers.

Owners of intellectual property are known as the *copyright owners*. They, or their agents, are the only people legally authorized to grant permission for others to copy their works. Copyright owners have agreed that, as their property is intangible, it can be effectively protected only by means of the law.

This is not a recent decision. The Stationers' Company Charter was granted through the Star Chamber Decree 1556. Less than 100 years later, the Star Chamber Decree 1637 provided that all books should be registered with the Company of Stationers. (Although its use is no longer a legal requirement, Stationers' Hall continues to maintain a register.) 280 years ago, the British Parliament announced the *Copyright Statute of Anne, 1709*. This basically covered books, printing and publishing, but various Acts from then on were introduced to cover such works as music, maps, engravings, sculpture, paintings, etc.

More recently, the 1911 Copyright Act repealed all of the previous Acts with only certain exceptions. This was followed by the 1956 Copyright Act, the 1971 Copyright (Amendment) Act and other related Acts, such as the 1949 Registered Designs Act, the 1958 Dramatic and Musical Performers Protection Act, the 1963 Performers' Protection Act, the 1968 Design Copyright Act and the 1972 Performers' Protection Act.

Leading copyright legislation into the 21st century, we now have the *Copyright, Designs and Patents Act 1988*. This basically restates the law of copyright and repeals previous legislation including the Copyright Act of 1956.

Many countries identify themselves with the United Kingdom by recognizing the necessity to provide severe penalties against those who are found guilty of infringement of copyright.

However, it is believed that many members of the general public are simply unaware of their rights and obligations under copyright legislation. One of the biggest obstacles is that of copyright owners and others either phrasing things in difficult-to-understand legalistic jargon, or else not actually making it clear that a work is protected by copyright. To help overcome this obstacle, this book has been written in everyday language in order to make available general, vital information on a highly complicated subject.

Prior to the 1988 Bill, Her Majesty's Government published a White Paper detailing proposals for changes in copyright legislation. Both individuals and organizations with an interest in copyright matters were able to make representations to the Government, through the Secretary of State for Trade and Industry, concerning the proposals. Of course, not everybody's whims could possibly be included in the new (now current) legislation. Nevertheless, the result is that the 1988 Act reflects current requirements appertaining to intellectual property ownership and should continue to do so for some time to come.

1
Definition and ownership _____

Every copyright owner has, in law, the exclusive right (restricted only by current legislation pertaining to libel, obscenity, and so on) to copy, translate, adapt, perform and/or publish, in any way he or she wishes, the work(s) that he or she owns. The law actually stipulates the length of time for which copyright of particular types of works will exist.

As soon as any idea has been translated into either a tangible or a retrievable format, a copyright has come into existence. For example, a songwriter records a new work onto magnetic tape, an author types out a manuscript, or a photographer takes a picture. These are examples of *tangible* formats of intellectual property. *Retrievable* formats are those (like computer programs) where information is stored electronically, but can be called up onto a screen or other display medium to be read.

In general, the copyright owner is the person (or persons) responsible for creating the work in the first instance. However, it is possible for another party to be, or to become, the copyright owner. This will normally happen when a work is commissioned. If you instruct a freelance author to write an essay on your behalf, then once you have paid for the author's services, all copyright in the finished essay is vested in yourself. As soon as you have paid the invoice rendered by your freelance acquaintance, the copyright in that essay is yours. To avoid any possible disagreement over this at a later date, it is essential to have an agreement drawn up in writing, if necessary by a solicitor. Note that the term of the copyright dates from the end of the calendar year in which the *original* author dies.

Another important example is work that is undertaken by an employee during the course of his employment. Any creative work you may produce for your employer automatically becomes the copyright of your employer unless you have an agreement to the contrary. The actual wording of the Act states that this applies to any work made by an employee "in the course of his employment". This leaves interpretation of the Act somewhat open in view of the fact that different employers and employees have differing guidelines as to what constitutes 'in the course of employment'.

The fine line is probably the one of normal working hours ending at 17.30 hours. You are just going through the door at 17.32 when your departmental head asks you to stay on and write a report that is required for a meeting next morning at 09.00. You could refuse, but he's a good employer and you're looking for promotion anyway. So, although there's no overtime pay, you stay on for a couple of hours to prepare the report. As this was done in your own time, even though you were utilizing your employer's lighting and heating, do you own the copyright in this report? Or was it prepared 'in the course of employment' so that the copyright belongs to your employer?

As the 1988 Act is still in its infancy, and only became law in 1989, there is still need for a test case to provide guidance on this delicate matter. I asked two employers how they viewed the situation. Interestingly enough, one felt that probably the copyright would belong, at least initially, to the employee. The second took a more cautious view and preferred to refrain from public comment! My feeling is that, until we are granted a more precise legal statement, through either a test case or a government statement, the ownership of the copyright must be agreed upon by both employer and employee in sensible discussion.

Intellectual property may be bought or sold in the same way as any other property. It is usual to refer to any such sale of copyright material as an *assignment* of copyright in any particular work. Sometimes authors assign their works to their publishers. All assignment arrangements should be agreed through a form of contract, such as an exchange of letters confirming the terms and conditions. Some copyright owners are not keen to relinquish their copyrights because, of course, they would then need permission to use their own work!

It is possible to license a publisher but retain copyright, e.g. an author may hold on to his copyright ownership but license a publisher to issue a particular edition of his book. During the period of such an agreement, the author would need permission from the publisher to use his work in many, if not all instances.

So it will be readily appreciated that, with only minor exceptions, the first copyright owner of any work is the creator of that work. The creator is often referred to as the *author*, although, dependent upon the type of work created, he could be the *composer, photographer, sculptor*, etc.

Period of copyright

Although copyright ownership takes effect from the moment an idea has been put into a tangible or retrievable form, it does not last indefinitely. For literature, music and pictures, copyright in Britain subsists for 50 years after the death of the author, composer or artist. This applies even if the original owner has assigned his/her copyright to another party, including a publishing or broadcasting company. In some European countries, copyright subsists until the end of the calendar year which falls other than 50 years after the author's death. These include Belgium (60 years), France (65 years), Federal Republic of Germany (70 years) and Italy (56 years).

If your copyright has been assigned to another person or a commercial company, the term of copyright *remains* as if you had retained your property.

Suppose, however, that you wrote something as part of your contract of employment with Pryntum Plc. The first owner of copyright in your work is legally your employer (unless you have an agreement that says otherwise). Is it correct, as some people have assumed, that the copyright expires only if Pryntum Plc closes down? No, because again the copyright subsists until that magical period of 50 years has passed following your decease.

But how does one actually know when something produced during employment, and thus the copyright of a business, is in or out of copyright? For certain categories of work, such as newspaper journalism, it should be possible to check back in the archives to ascertain when a piece was written, or at least published, and by whom it was written. But many items, such as reports, technical data, tables and so on, *appear* to have been produced anonymously.

Unless a record has been kept, detailing every piece of company copyright output, including authors, dates prepared, etc., one can only assume that such documents have been prepared anonymously. In such cases, the term of copyright is exactly the same as, for example, an anthology of poems by an anonymous poet; the copyright expires at the end of the calendar year that falls 50 years after the date when the work was first made available to the public. As most company documents are dated in some way, this should present no problem. However, it could be argued that a document prepared privately and confidentially for the sole use of the board of directors had never been made available to the public, in which case the copyright would still be vested in the company.

The major exception to this rule is when a work is created by the Queen or any of her servants in the course of their employment. In such works, Her Majesty is always the initial owner of the copyright, and such works are designated to be in *Crown copyright*. Crown copyright exists until the end of the calendar year which falls 125 years from the year in which the work was created. However, should a Crown copyright work be commercially published within 75 years of the date it was created, the copyright expires at the end of the calendar year that falls 50 years from the date of such publication.

Different arrangements apply to cinematograph films, video tapes, audio tapes, audio records, compact discs, computer programs, etc. The copyright term for these media is 50 years from the date when any such item is first made available to the public. It is becoming increasingly common practice for publishers to print on their packaging of these items the symbol ℗ followed by the year of publication. The ℗ simply stands for the word *published*, and by adding 50 to the publication year you can easily note when the copyright in that published item expires. It is important to remember that this applies only to the copyright of the publishing method used, e.g. in the case of an audio tape it would be the copyright in the original sound recording; the actual work recorded will still be in copyright if its originator is still alive, or died less than 50 years previously. Of course, any completely fresh recording of a work enjoys a completely fresh 50 year period of copyright.

International copyright

In a strict literal sense, there is no such thing as international copyright. However in practice, copyright protection is afforded in all of the main areas around the globe, thanks primarily to a couple of major conventions. In the first instance, copyright protection is guaranteed in an individual country through the laws of that country. Countries that have signed the *Berne Convention* (1886 and later revisions) have each agreed to extend the benefits of their own national copyright laws to citizens of all other member-nations. No registration nor claim is required. Copyright owners also have the benefit of a moral right to object to any alterations in their work(s). More than 80 countries are signatories to the Berne Convention.

The *Universal Copyright Convention* (1952) also boasts more than 80 signatures. As with the Berne Convention, member-nations afford the benefit of their own national copyright legislation to citizens of other member-nations. Under the Universal Copyright Convention, all works claiming copyright protection must display the UCC symbol ©, the name of the copyright owner, and the year of publication.

The main difference between the Berne and the Universal Conventions is that the Berne treaty actually stipulates minimum standards of copyright protection which each member country must include in its own copyright legislation, whereas the Universal treaty sets out no such conditions. Both conventions contain special concessionary provisions which developing countries may include in their own national legislation. It is interesting to note that approximately 50 countries are members of both copyright conventions. A list of all members is given in Appendix 6.

In view of the fact that so many countries are signatories to both conventions, it will be readily appreciated that a good proportion of the copyright laws of such member-nations run in parallel. To check up on the exact rights conferred in law by any particular country will necessitate reading up the copyright legislation of that country. If this should prove necessary, information *may* be available at the main reference library in your area. Otherwise, you could enquire of that country's embassy or other official representation, or write to the British Copyright Council (address in Appendix 2).

Registration of copyright

Under the Berne Convention, no specific registration is called for, nor is any claim to copyright ownership required. Under the Universal Copyright Convention, all copyright works must display the symbol ©. Until recent times, it was necessary to register copyright works in the United States of America, but this requirement is now being phased out, and new works do not require any registration.

Although the international copyright symbol © does appear on the majority, if not all, of commercially published works, some schools of thought hold that it is not completely necessary since in law any person(s) wishing to use a work, in any way and for any purpose, should take all reasonable steps to check whether or not that work is in copyright and, if it is, to obtain the necessary permission or licence. However, as the symbol assists copyright owners to make it clear that their works are in live copyright, it is an increasing practice to display the symbol on virtually any copyright work.

Recently, the symbol © has been enjoying a growing familiarity within the advertising world and on grocery labels. But beware! The fact that some item or work happens to have the symbol © imprinted on it does not serve to prove any specific copyright ownership; the symbol may have been incorrectly applied.

Copyright in a particular work may not necessarily be vested in one individual or one concern (such as a publishing company). For example, if a play has been written jointly by two playwrights, the finished work (unless assigned to another party) would have the copyright vested in both of their names. Where a work is owned by more than one party, permission to use it would need to be granted by all of the parties enjoying a share of the copyright, although in practice it is generally the publisher who grants such permissions, acting as agent for the copyright owners.

It is to be borne in mind that the term of copyright expires at the end of the calendar year which comes 50 years after the death of an author. Where a work has more than one author, the individual items written by each author attract a separate copyright. For some items, the copyrights are easy to separate, e.g. a song with words by a lyricist and music by a composer. If the lyricist dies this year, then copyright in the words will expire in 50 years time. If the composer died 53 years ago, then the music has already been out of copyright ownership for three years.

In the previous example of a drama written jointly by two playwrights, unless the playwrights have each written complete and distinct scenes and/or acts, there may be some difficulty in distinguishing which parts of the play each playwright can claim copyright ownership of. However, commonsense must always prevail, and in this particular instance it is unlikely that anyone would wish to reproduce parts of a play simply because the copyright in those parts has expired due to the playwright having deceased over five decades ago. A play is a play and is intended to be viewed in its entirety. Consequently, anybody wishing to reproduce a play or similar work of joint authorship would normally wait until all copyrights involved had expired.

So, with no official registration procedures, and no genuine obligation to even portray the international copyright symbol, many copyright owners have rightly been concerned over the vexed question of proving their ownership of intellectual works. The debate has, thus far, resigned itself to the inevitable conclusion that it is improbable that any particular copyright ownership could actually be proved conclusively and without the remotest doubt. Fortunately, however, there does exist a selection of ways to prove, beyond reasonable doubt, that a particular work was actually *in existence* upon a given date.

A common method is for a copyright owner to post a copy of their work(s) by registered mail to themselves. The envelope would need to be identified in some way so that there is some method of remembering exactly what material is contained in it. Once the Post Office has delivered the package, it should be retained *unopened* until it becomes necessary to prove copyright ownership, e.g. in a court of law. In court, the postmark will prove that the work was in existence upon the date of posting. To ensure that the unopened envelope is kept safely after delivery, it is suggested that such items be deposited at a bank, and a receipt obtained.

An obvious way of saving both time and money is to abbreviate

the method outlined in the previous paragraph. By simply taking your sealed package to your bank for deposit, and obtaining a clearly dated receipt which identifies the packet in question, e.g. by quoting a coded reference that you have written on the packet to identify the contents, the bank receipt should serve to prove that your work was in existence at the date of deposit. However, many people prefer to double up the checks by sending the packet to themselves by registered mail. This method provides double evidence, and ensures that they could not be accused of possibly coming up with an envelope that was only claimed to have been deposited at a bank.

An alternative to registered post is the Royal Mail Recorded Delivery service. However, some authorities believe that registered post is the service that would be considered favourably by a court, which suggests that the more expensive service is the one to go for. As with registered post, the postmark on a recorded delivery package will serve only to prove that the contents were in existence upon the date of posting.

In days now long past there was a legal obligation for copyright owners to register their works at the Stationers' Hall Copyright Registry in Ludgate Hill. Although this requirement ceased on 31 December 1923, the Stationers' Hall continued to maintain a copyright register. Copyright owners may voluntarily apply to have their work listed within this register. The charge in 1988 was £20 per entry (plus VAT), plus an additional £10 (plus VAT) for a certified copy of the entry. All entries in the Stationers' Hall Register are destroyed after seven years without reference to copyright owners. Those who do not wish their entries to be destroyed are obliged to inform Stationers' Hall accordingly, and pay a further registration fee every seven years. It is pertinent to note that all entries in the Stationers' Hall Register are intended for record purposes only, and for assisting in the proof of existence of a work upon the date of registration.

A further method of establishing the existence of a particular work upon a given date would be for a copyright owner to take a copy of their work to a Commissioner for Oaths, and swear that it was their own originally created work. The cost of such a swearing would reflect the professional fees applicable at the time.

All that I have said so far has assumed a copyright work that has been translated into a tangible form, e.g. prose or poetry written down, or a musical work recorded onto audio tape, or a theatrical production recorded onto video tape. But what about an intangible form of copyright? How would somebody prove the existence, on a certain date, of a *retrievable work*, the most common of which is probably a computer program?

This is almost certainly one of the most difficult areas within the whole spectrum of copyright legalistics. The obvious answer – to produce a hard copy – is, regrettably, not often as easy as it may seem. Where it is possible to produce a hard copy, the copyright owner has produced a tangible form of their work, and may proceed as before to establish the existence of the work.

If a program has been saved onto a disk or computer tape, it is a relatively simple matter to make a duplicate disk or tape. The duplicate may then be treated as a tangible work.

In the case of an intangible work which for some reason may only be retrieved onto a visual display unit, the proper course of action is to display the main features of the work on the screen, and have photographs taken which may together be treated as tangible.

Some care is needed to take a satisfactory off-screen picture and professional assistance may be necessary. Any camera that will give an aperture of f4 and a shutter speed down to around 1/10 second should be suitable. A picture on the screen of a television set is produced from two sets of interlaced lines. Each scans the picture in 1/50 second, so it takes 1/25 second to produce a complete picture. A purpose made computer VDU may form its complete picture in a shorter time, but nevertheless an exposure longer than 1/50 second may be required to get the complete picture. A camera on a steady tripod and some trial exposures will be necessary.

Moral rights

Under UK copyright legislation, every copyright owner has the moral right to be identified. So the author of a literary or dramatic work, or the composer of a musical score, or the director of a film, has the full backing of British law enforcement should they wish to claim their moral right to be suitably identified. Moral rights apply when a work is published commercially, performed in public, broadcast or otherwise made available.

Although moral rights are wide-ranging including, for example, that an architect has the right to be identified in relation to a building he has designed, the moral right does *not* apply to the author of a computer program, nor to the designer of a typeface. Other important exceptions include items for publication in such productions as newspapers and magazines, encyclopedias, dictionaries, yearbooks and similar collective works. Items produced in the normal course of employment where the employer is the first owner of copyright are also excepted.

Additionally, the moral right does not apply to the use of a copyright work, when that particular use would not infringe copyright in that work, e.g. fair dealing or inclusion in academic examination questions (see page 22).

An important facet of moral right is that the author of a literary, dramatic, musical or artistic work, or the director of a copyright film, may claim the right not to have their work subjected to 'unjustified modification' for the purposes of publication or performance.

Conversely, a person also has the right to object to a work being falsely attributed to them for whatever reason.

Moral rights subsist for as long as a work remains in copyright, with the exception that the right to object to false attribution subsists only until 20 years following a person's death.

It is an important consideration to be borne in mind, that the moral right is retained by authors, or other creators of copyright works, for the entire period in which their works are protected by copyright, i.e. until the end of the calendar year which falls 50 years from their decease. Suppose, for instance, that you have illustrated the book *Fruits of my Brain Child* by Gildie Leaves. Your name is Greye Selles. Under your moral right, you may insist that the publisher prints on the cover and/or title page of the book words to the effect of 'Illustrated by Greye Selles'. This applies even if you have sold or assigned your copyright to the book's publishers. If you happen to be employed by the publishers and have illustrated the book as part of your employment contract, you could *not* claim this right.

In exercising your right to be identified as the illustrator of the book (this moral right is often described as the *right of paternity*) you also have the right to object to 'derogatory treatment' of your work (and this moral right is frequently cited as the *right of integrity*). Unlike the property style of ownership in the copyright of your work, the rights of paternity and integrity *cannot* be sold or assigned in any way. Rather 'ethereal' in nature, these rights are personal to you. The only way these rights may become someone else's property is by your death; you are perfectly free to pass on your right of paternity and your right of integrity via your last will and testament.

The 1988 Act insists that an author wishing to implement their right of paternity must assert their desire in writing. Presumably reputable publishers help their authors by including a suitable clause in their publishing agreements. Otherwise, you can waive your moral rights by an exchange of letters or other form of written agreement (e.g. a clause in your contract) with your publisher.

Whilst on the subject of book publishing, it's worth mentioning that most, if not all, publishers have come across the occasional author who objects strongly to the slightest alteration to their manuscript. Minor editorial alterations for the purpose of publication could not possibly be described as 'unjustified modification'. However, to cover themselves legally, more and more publishers are now writing into their contracts with authors a clause which gives them (the publishers) the right to editorial modifications which, in the publishers' view, are necessary for the success of the final published work.

Adaptations and arrangements of copyright works

The 1988 Act declares that it is an infringement of copyright in a literary, dramatic or musical work to make any adaptation or arrangement without the prior consent of the copyright owner.

Adaptation includes translating a literary work, converting it into a play (or a play into a story), converting a story into a pictorial sequence, recording the work in writing or otherwise, and so on. In cases of computer programs, conversion into a different computer language except in the incidental course of running the program is included. In the case of a musical work, any arrangement or transcription comes into this category.

However unfair it may seem, it would appear that, when an adaptation or arrangement is made of a copyright work, any copyright in the new arrangement becomes the property of the owner of the original work. On the other hand, an adaptation or arrangement of a non-copyright work becomes the copyright of the person responsible for the new arrangement or adaptation.

It is generally accepted that there is no copyright protection of a title or of fictitious characters created by an author. However it may well be possible to create *merchandising rights* in suitable characters.

The Copyright Tribunal

With legislation as complex as copyright is, it is inevitable that disputes will arise from time to time. Under the 1956 Copyright Act, *The Tribunal* was established as a body empowered to attempt to settle such disputes. In section 145 of the Copyright, Designs and Patents Act 1988, that tribunal is given a new name, the *Copyright Tribunal*.

The Copyright Tribunal has a chairman and two deputy chairmen, each appointed by the Lord Chancellor in the light of discussions with the Lord Advocate. It should also have a minimum of two and a maximum of eight 'ordinary members' appointed by the Secretary of State. Persons holding the senior posts of chairman and deputy chairmen are required to be barristers, advocates or solicitors with at least seven years' experience, or persons who can claim to have held a judicial post.

As a legal body, the Copyright Tribunal is empowered to hear a variety of cases in which a copyright dispute has arisen. However, the major proceedings expected are concerned with disputes concerning copyright licensing schemes, royalties payable in respect of the rental of audio recordings, films and computer programs, and royalties or other payments to the Hospital for Sick Children.

Should a defendant be unhappy with a ruling of the Copyright Tribunal, an appeal may be made to the High Court (in Scotland, such appeals should be directed to the Court of Session).

2
Photocopying and duplication _____

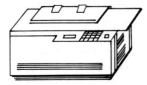

Major advances in reprographics technology in recent years, and wholesale flaunting of the copyright laws, have resulted in some considerable losses of income by many copyright owners. The situation is such that some people have been totally misled into believing that they may actually have the right to copy pages from books and magazines!

Copyright legislation does, however, provide that it is *not* an infringement to make a single copy of a literary, dramatic, musical or artistic work for the express purposes of research or private study. For such purposes, therefore, it is not necessary to seek prior permission from copyright owners or agents. Note, also, that there is no infringement of any typographical arrangement copyright (see later) in respect of photocopying for research or private study. It is imperative to note that this provision applies generally to single copies of a work being reproduced for genuine cases of *research* and *private study*. A teacher running off a class set of an article could not claim immunity under this provision, nor could a member of the local women's club claim immunity for running off copies of a recipe from one of the weekly magazines; nor a bandmaster making copies of a popular tune; nor a choirmaster making copies of a song.

The availability of copying for research and private study purposes is cited as a *fair dealing* provision. This clearly implies that any copying under this provision should be restricted to the extract(s) of a work that are needed for the study and/or research being undertaken. It is unlikely, for example, that the copying of journal articles in full was ever envisaged.

As a gesture of goodwill, the Society of Authors and the Publishers Association jointly announced in 1965 that they would, on behalf of their members, go one step further than the law required. Some photocopying of their members' works would be permitted without the need to obtain permission or pay any licence or other fees. In the case of a book or article, single copies could be made of one extract up to 4000 words in length, or a series of extracts could be copied provided that each extract did not exceed 3000 words, and the total of the series of extracts did not amount to more than 8000 words. There was a further restriction, in that in any instance of copying, the actual permitted maximum should not exceed 10 per cent of the work being copied. This 'kind offer' was never extended to cover such things as poems, essays, short works, music and journal articles, for which permission to copy has always been required.

Sadly, however, as so often happens, the dispensation granted by the two organizations was more and more widely flouted. As reprographics technology advanced, as copying machinery became common office furniture, and instant print shops sprang up all over the country, so illicit photocopying and printing increased. Many offenders quoted in justification the document *Photocopying and the Law*, which was the published version of the joint Society of Authors and Publishers Association statement. Consequently, in March 1985, the joint statement was withdrawn and no longer applies under any circumstances.

There are now two photocopying licensing organizations: the Christian Music Association, which deals with music used mainly in churches, and the Copyright Licensing Agency, which deals with more general use of copyright material published in books (excluding certain items, including music). The services of these agencies are explained later in this chapter, although it may be noted now that the CLA licence, being general in character, has been designed to include limited multiple copying as is often required for educational and industrial use.

Another relaxation of the restrictions applies to single copies of copyright material that may be photocopied without infringing copyright for the requirements of *judicial proceedings*. Remember that any copies produced, for any reason, should always carry some kind of credit reference, e.g. 'From *See for Yourself*, copyright 1985, Jay Books'.

Statutory Instrument 1957, No. 868, gives details of certain prescribed libraries who are authorized by the Department of Trade and Industry to make copies of copyright works so long as certain conditions can be fulfilled. As a general rule, the libraries in question are non-profit making. The conditions to be complied with are:

- The person requesting the copy signs a statutory declaration and undertaking to the effect that the copy requested is only to be used for the purposes of research and/or private study.

- Where journal articles are involved, only one article may be copied from any one publication.

- The prescribed library must charge 'not less than the cost (including a contribution to the general expenses of the library) attributable to the production' of the photocopying work undertaken.

- Where copying of items other than journal articles is involved, copying must be restricted to a 'reasonable proportion' of the work(s).

- Where copying of items other than journal articles is involved, no copying may be undertaken if the librarian knows the name and address of a person who is able to authorize copying. Nor may a copy be made if the librarian could through reasonable enquiries obtain the name and address of such a person.

This final provision means effectively that no copy should be made of any copyright work currently in print (other than journal articles), because the name and address of the publisher will be included in the published edition of any such work.

In educational circles, there has been some debate as to whether schools and colleges may undertake unauthorized photocopying without infringing copyright. In fact the law is quite clear: copies of a work may be produced in educational institutions, but only if the copies produced form part of an examination question paper.

As part of a course of instruction in an educational establishment, however, copies may be made by either a teacher or a student on condition that no duplicating process of any kind (including photocopying) is employed. Thus, it is permissible for a teacher to write an extract of a copyright work onto a chalkboard or whiteboard, for example, and for pupils to copy this into their exercise books.

Multiple copying

In order to undertake legally any multiple copying, or to undertake any copying not covered by the legal exclusions outlined above, it is necessary to obtain permission from the copyright owner (or their agent) in advance. Permission should always be obtained in writing. If you do not know the name and address of the copyright owner, write to the publishers, whose name and address is usually printed on the back of the title page of a book, or at the foot of the first page of a magazine. In many instances, it will be discovered that the publisher is the agent for granting permission anyway.

There is another reason why it might be better to write to the publisher first in each and every case. The actual typography and artwork of every publication has a separate copyright from the work itself. The work is the intellectual property of its owner, i.e. its author, composer or artist. But the typography and design of a published edition commands a special *typographical copyright*, which is owned by the publisher and lasts for 25 years from the date of first publication.

Suppose you wish to photocopy two pages from a book. The copyright is owned by the author so far as the intellectual work is concerned, and this copyright subsists until 50 years after his death. You would need the permission of the author (or his heir) to photocopy his intellectual work. However, the book has been published by Jay Books, and they own the typographical copyright which subsists until the book has been around for 25 years. You would need their permission to copy their typographical work. The chances are that Jay Books also act on behalf of their authors, so one letter to them, as publishers, could obtain the two permissions that you actually require.

It is easy to overlook the existence of typographical copyright. Although you may know that an author or composer has been dead for more than 50 years, you may still need permission to photocopy something from a published edition of his work. It is usual for publishers to indicate the year of publication on the back of the title page. Check that the particular edition has been around for at least 25 years. If it has been published more recently than this, then you will certainly need the publisher's permission!

If you undertake a lot of multiple photocopying on behalf of an educational, commercial or religious establishment, you will almost certainly find it helpful to subscribe to one of two blanket licensing schemes. The Copyright Licensing Agency controls the blanket licensing for most commercial and educational photocopying, while the Christian Music Association maintains a copyright licence scheme covering certain categories of church music. Their addresses are given in Appendix 2.

Copyright Licensing Agency scheme

Over a decade ago, the Whitford Committee recommended the establishment of a general body to oversee matters pertaining to photocopying. As a direct result of this recommendation, the Copyright Licensing Agency was set up. The agency was incorporated in 1983, sponsored by the Authors' Lending and Copyright Society together with the Publishers' Licensing Society. Between them, these two organizations represent the Society of Authors, the Writers' Guild of Great Britain, the Association of Authors' Agents, the Publishers Association, the Periodical Publishers Association and the Association of Learned and Professional Society Publishers.

The Copyright Licensing Agency (CLA) serves as a national clearing centre through which the owners and users of copyright books and serials can deal with each other more or less automatically when permissions and royalties are required. The agency enables both organizations and individuals to comply with the law, and is a single-source authorization and payment house for the copiers of such copyright work.

CLA has been justly described as a "balancing mechanism between competing needs" in that it is totally committed to providing its users with the least burdensome means for obtaining authorizations for copying, yet it is equally committed to obtaining a fair recompense for that copying for authors and publishers alike.

Basically, any person or organization, of any description, that happens to own (or rent) a photocopying machine may obtain a CLA photocopying licence. This licence is renewable annually, and allows the copying of up to five per cent of a book (except in the case of one short story or one poem from a collection, which may be copied in its entirety provided it does not exceed ten pages), and the whole or part of one article from a periodical, journal or magazine, or other serial.

It is inevitable that the CLA licence does *not* cover the photocopying of certain works, for which individual permission to copy is still required. These are:

- printed music (including the words),
- test or examination papers,
- industrial house journals,
- newspapers,
- privately owned documents,
- maps, charts, tabulations,
- workbooks, workcards, assignment sheets,
- separate photographs and/or illustrations,
- bibles, liturgical works, orders of service sheets.

It is advisable always to check individual works (in the case of books, refer to the reverse of the title page) lest a special notice has been incorporated stating that the work is excluded from the CLA scheme.

Some publishers have specific works that cannot be included in the CLA scheme for individual and particular reasons. A list of these, correct at the time of going to press, is included in Appendix 4.

Apart from the exceptions indicated above, the advantage of the CLA licence is that it does enable legal copying of a majority of items with an original UK imprint, thus removing the necessity of, and work involved with, having to seek prior permission on each occasion.

The Copyright Licensing Agency is a member of the International Forum for Reprographic Rights Organizations, and is actively pursuing negotiations with countries outside the UK with a view to setting up reciprocal agreements. Such moves are to be encouraged because the ultimate aim is for members of the CLA scheme to receive automatic permission to photocopy works originating outside the UK, and to be administered (for photocopying purposes) by the corresponding organizations in other countries.

The CLA have so far pulled off such reciprocal agreements with both the United States of America and France, and are expecting to secure reciprocal arrangements with other countries including Germany, Italy, The Netherlands and Spain.

It is important to stress that the CLA licence does *not* permit unlimited copying of any copyright material; nor does it replace any copyright legislation, so any infringement of copyright caused through copying outside of the terms of the licence may still lead to prosecution. For educational requirements, teachers may make copies for each member of a class to use for personal use or study, plus one copy for the teacher or lecturer's own use.

Educational bodies were the first to recognize the advantages of subscribing to the CLA scheme on a corporate scale, thus CLA operates a collective licensing arrangement so that local education authorities may take out a collective licence for the schools and colleges under their wing. Other groups of institutions may also take out collective licences. Concerns that do not have a parent body to take out a collective licence may take out their own transactional licence.

Following in the footsteps of their educational counterparts, the 'trade, industry and commerce' fraternal are now beginning to take out CLA licences on a wide scale. This fraternal spans the entire commercial spectrum from the Times Top 500 Companies through to the popular high street copyshops.

Perhaps this interest was sparked off by the fact that in recent times, specifically noticeable since the early 1980s, violators of the copyright laws have been discovering that getting prosecuted hurts their pockets. Not only are the interested pressure groups pushing for the heaviest penalties now, but some cases have attracted the additional punishment of adverse publicity. As a direct result of the 1988 Copyright, Designs and Patents Act, stiffer penalties will almost certainly be awarded against offenders in the future. Incidentally, some cases have been brought to attention well after an offence was alleged to have been committed, and such cases act as timely reminders that a summons in respect of infringement of copyright may be lodged at any time up to and including six years from the date of the alleged infringement.

To make it abundantly clear to users of photocopying machines at those establishments holding a Copyright Licensing Agency agreement exactly what they are entitled to copy (and not to copy!), CLA provide a notice for display on or beside copying machines. This provides instant, though necessarily brief but straightforward, guidelines as to the scope of the CLA licence. A space is provided for establishments to incorporate on the notice the name of a person to be contacted should any user of the photocopying machine have any doubts or queries involving any item to be copied.

In any cases where doubt arises, the chances are that special permission to copy needs to be obtained. Remember: if in doubt, check it out!

Educational copying

Contrary to some popular schools of thought, copying for teaching purposes is unlawful unless prior permission has been obtained from the copyright owners. The main exception to this rule is where a school has a CLA licence and undertakes its copying within the terms of that licence.

In order to ensure that authors and publishers receive fair rewards for their works which are copied under the CLA scheme, records need to be kept of exactly what is being copied and how frequently. This would be an onerous task for individual teachers. So, for reasons of practicality, where a local education authority has taken out a blanket licence for its schools and colleges, a few establishments only are selected each academic year to maintain full records of all their photocopying output of copyright material. These records are then used as the basis for determining the extent of copying within each educational area.

Special record forms are issued to those schools and colleges selected, and it is intended that these forms should be completed at the actual time of any photocopying taking place. The type of information required includes the number of pages copied (part of a page counting as a full page), the actual number of copies made, the title of the book, periodical or journal and its International Standard Book Number (ISBN) or International Standard Serial Number (ISSN) as appropriate, the name of the author or the issue date of the periodical or journal and, in the case of books only, the name of the publisher. Records do not have to be completed for those items where separate permission has been obtained from the copyright owner, copying of items not covered by the CLA licence, copyright free material, etc.

Should any local authorities not have a current CLA licence, then the schools and colleges under their wing would be well advised to take out their own individual licences. Indeed, this is what independent schools and colleges are encouraged to do as they have no umbrella organization that can take out a blanket licence to cover them.

Future CLA schemes

With the advent of the Copyright, Designs and Patents Act 1988, the Copyright Licensing Agency has found itself in a position from which it needs to forge ahead, developing new licence schemes to cover different categories of users of reprographics including not only photocopiers, but laser printers, facsimile machines, computers, slides, overhead projector transparencies, lithographic printing, and the rest. During the currency of this book, the CLA will be debating whether or not to introduce schemes tailor-made to cover the following types of users: government and public bodies; libraries; trade, industry and commerce; others (e.g. charities and churches).

CMA copyright licence scheme

This scheme has been devised for churches and other groups who wish to photocopy the words of religious songs, or write them onto overhead projector transparencies, for temporary use by their congregations. To join the scheme, a fee is payable annually, and the sum is calculated upon the number of people, on average, attending the main services of the church.

A number of religious music publishers have lent their names to the scheme, and churches taking out the annual licence are authorized to use the words only of songs which have the copyright vested in the names of any of the participating publishers.

Many publishers of religious music are known to grant permission for the words of songs to be reproduced free of charge, for use in such temporary formats as an ohp transparency. It may be presumed, therefore, that some publishers supporting this scheme are amongst those who would normally charge a royalty for the use of their works. It must be emphasized that this particular scheme does only cover works of which the copyright is controlled by the participating publishers.

Organizations considering joining the scheme should consider whether or not the licence fee represents money well spent. If they are likely to use only one or two pieces each year from the publishers

Permission to make one copy does not mean one copy per member.

in this scheme, it would probably be far cheaper to seek individual permissions than to take out the blanket licence.

A list of the various copyright owners and music publishers associated with the scheme and the publications and songbooks involved are given in Appendix 5.

The Christian Music Association scheme is such that its scope extends to writing out the words of songs on posters or other large sheets, blackboards, whiteboards and similar products. Interestingly, the scheme also specifically includes electronic means of visual reproduction – looking ahead, no doubt, to the days when churches will boast their own closed circuit television systems. As far as photocopying of hymns is concerned, the CMA licence provides for "photocopies of authorized worship songs from authorized music books for musicians to compile a personal music folio and index in alphabetical order where the musician has personally purchased the authorized music book(s) concerned". Individual arrangements of musical parts for particular instruments may also be photocopied subject to the condition that a copy of each is furnished to the original publisher(s).

The CMA licence does only cover material to be used in connection with Christian services of divine worship in Britain and Ireland. So if you are a teacher wishing to use the words of a Christian song to illustrate a point in your religious instruction class, you would probably not qualify for a CMA licence to cover running off a class set. In this example, you might be covered by the Copyright Licensing Agency scheme anyway; if not, then apply to the publisher for permission.

Note also that under the CMA scheme, the reproduced material may be used only by the licence holder, and no admission or other charge may be made for the event. Full acknowledgement must be made, and a copy of all printed material supplied to the association.

Music Publishers' Association

The copying of music is particularly prevalent in the religious area. For many years, most hymns used in churches were from earlier generations and therefore in the public domain as far as copyright was concerned. The rapid growth of 'worship songs' in recent years has radically changed all that. Now the majority of songs are in copyright.

The Music Publishers' Association receives a constant flow of enquiries regarding religious music and photocopying by churches and other religious organizations, and, at the risk of repetition, it is worth repeating a statement that they have issued on behalf of their various members.

Copyright is infringed if a work is reproduced in a tangible form, such as by photocopying, or arranged in any way. There have already been two cases involving legal action against church choirs, and copyright owners are entitled to sue for damages against those who copy. Many gospel songs are fully copyright and cannot be photocopied without permission.

If you are in any doubt at all about the copyright status of the words or music you are using you should check with the copyright owner who is usually the publisher mentioned at the bottom of the page of the songbook or hymn book, *not* the publisher of the collection. If you have difficulty in tracing a copyright owner please contact the Music Publishers' Association who may be able to assist.

The fundamental principle adopted by the Music Publishers' Association is that any copying to evade purchase is wrong. It is not only immoral but also uneconomic in the long run as any choir which photocopies for its members is having its music unfairly subsidized by those who are adhering to the law. If a copying permission is required and you know the work is copyright, prior written application should always be made to the copyright owner. It's safer and your conscience will be clear! Remember, photocopying can have a drastic effect in reducing songbooks purchased by churches thus creating a vicious circle by ultimately affecting the number of hymns, etc., available in published form.

Special items

Examination questions

All questions included in examination papers are the copyright of the examining boards, whose names are always printed on their relevant question papers. If you wish to photocopy any examination paper, or even just a selection of questions from it, you should first write to the examining board to seek the appropriate permission.

Some examining boards publish a leaflet outlining copyright information, conditions of use, and so on, relevant to their publications. A prime example is the leaflet *Copyright on Board Publications: Note to Authors and Publishers*, issued by the Associated Examining Board, Stag Hill House, Guildford, Surrey, GU2 5XJ.

Overhead projector transparencies

For copyright purposes, it is generally reckoned that projecting an overhead projector transparency to a group of people is equivalent to letting each of them have a photocopied version of whatever they see on the screen.

Consequently, any copyright material you wish to include on an ohp acetate should be treated in similar fashion to photocopying. Prior permission in writing should be obtained from the copyright owner, with the exception of any copyright licensing scheme that you may subscribe to which expressly includes the making of ohp transparencies in its terms.

Ordnance Survey publications

Maps and charts published by the Ordnance Survey are of a

particular interest (from the point of view of photocopying) to representatives of selected professions. To meet this demand, the Ordnance Survey issues licences directly to solicitors, estate agents, architects, printers and other users.

The private copier

Anybody who undertakes any amount of photocopying may join either or both of the blanket licensing schemes discussed earlier in this chapter. However, these schemes, for practical reasons, are really designed for the person or organization who is undertaking a considerable amount of copying.

Those of us who have a need to make only a handful of copies now and then are better advised to apply to copyright owners, or their agents, as and when we desire to make the copies. For private use, I have found that in the majority of cases permission is freely given, subject only to a suitable credit acknowledgement being written or typed onto the relevant photocopies. For the price of a stamp, and the courtesy of a stamped, self-addressed envelope for the reply, this is well worth the minor trouble involved in writing. I suspect that copyright owners would not be quite so kindhearted if they discovered some copies lying around for which no prior permission had been granted!

When writing to copyright owners (if you don't know the actual name and/or address write c/o the publishers of whatever you wish to copy) it will save you, and them, a lot of time and effort if you remember to provide the details that they will require to know before they are able to grant any permissions. These may seem to be such obvious requirements, but it is surprising just how often people forget to mention something! So here's a handy check list for you:

- Your name and address, together with your daytime telephone number if you have one.

- The title of the work you wish to copy and, in the case of a book, the actual page numbers.

- The actual number of photocopies you wish to make.

- The purpose for which the photocopies will be made.

- If the copies are to be made on behalf of an organization, the name and address of that organization.

- If you are intending to distribute photocopies to other people, e.g. members of your club, you must state whether or not those people will be charged for their copies. If a charge is to be made, you must state whether this is purely the cost of producing the photocopies, or if some profit is to be made from the sale of the photocopies.

- Any other information that you think is pertinent to your application.

If you are addressing your application to the publisher of the work you wish to photocopy, remember to ask also for special permission to photocopy from the published book or other publication. Remember that the publishers have a separate copyright in the typographical layout of their production.

If you are seeking permission from a party that is not also the publisher, then, once you have obtained permission to photocopy the intellectual work, you must write to the publisher to obtain that separate permission in respect of the typographical copyright. In such instances, remember to make it clear to the publishers that you already have permission in respect of the intellectual copyright.

The international scene

Although the Copyright Licensing Agency issues blanket licences within the United Kingdom, it is pleasing to note that similar schemes either exist, or are in the course of being created, in many other countries. In the United States of America, the Copyright Clearance Center looks after the interests of copyright owners in respect of photocopying; there are also schemes in Australia, Austria, France, the Netherlands, Switzerland and West Germany. The UK Copyright Licensing Agency has initiated negotiations with some of these countries, with a view to securing reciprocal agreements on reprography. In the long term it is hoped that the many subscribers to the Copyright Licensing Agency scheme will be able to enjoy the benefits of a truly international reciprocal arrangement.

It cannot be denied that illegal photocopying is nothing less than outright theft. It has been suggested that, in some institutions, reprographics machinery is considerably overworked – producing illicit copies of all manner of documentation. It is universally agreed by agents acting on behalf of copyright owners that many members of the general public photocopy articles from magazines, or pages from books, using the photocopiers at their local libraries or other public establishments, without having the slightest twinge of a guilty conscience. When they are approached and caught in the act, a common response is: 'everybody does it and it doesn't harm anybody'.

This idle view reflects on the tip of the iceberg of international piracy, and is such a serious matter that, in 1986, the British Government's Foreign and Commonwealth Office issued a circular to all UK posts overseas. This memorandum spelt out the damage being done to United Kingdom trade by such piracy, and concluded by setting out ways in which diplomatic missions should work for effective protection of UK works.

Professional bodies

A number of professional bodies represent the needs of their members as far as copyright is concerned. Many of these are constituent bodies of the British Copyright Council. One of the tasks that many of these organizations perform is that of pursuing various methods of informing the general public to consider carefully whether or not they need permission before photocopying something. They will happily answer any questions put to them, and you will find their addresses in Appendix 2.

Public photocopiers

It is not in the least surprising that copyright owners view the high street copyshops and the installation of public photocopiers in libraries, post offices, petrol stations, etc., with some concern.

In the case of the copyshops, it is not unusual for customers to have to declare that they have obtained any necessary copyright permission prior to placing an order for instant printing or copying. Such shops have terms of business, available for inspection upon request, that include a clause to this effect. Such conditions are desirable, lest the copyshop ever be cited for aiding and abetting an act of copyright infringement.

It is rather more difficult to control what matter is copied on a self-service coin-in-the-slot public photocopier. In most places where there is a public photocopier, notices are displayed which briefly inform the users of these machines of their obligations under the copyright laws. However, as these machines are not individually supervised, it is suspected that many customers simply disregard the warning notices. Such customers are asked not to photocopy anything they haven't obtained permission to use; apart from clearly breaking the law and risking heavy penalties, the owner or operator of the photocopier could well be cited for aiding and abetting.

Using photocopied material

It should be appreciated that it is against the law to *knowingly* have and/or use any copies of any copyright work that have been produced without the prior permission of the copyright owner. There is a sense in which knowingly using an infringing copy is also aiding and abetting the infringer! Stiffer penalties than ever before are now being dealt out to those found guilty of knowingly using infringing copies. It has been suggested that church congregations may well rank among the worse offenders, so if you attend church services, weddings, youth organizations, etc., you are advised to check that the duplicated or photocopied song or hymn sheet has been produced with the permission(s) of the copyright owner(s)!

Should you have any reason whatsoever to suspect that documents in your possession could be infringing copyright you should check with the source of these documents. If that is not possible, you could have a word with your local Trading Standards Officer who may be able to offer help and advice.

Facsimile transmission

High fidelity technology has produced for us a simple and relatively cheap method of letting our friends and business acquaintances, wherever they may be, have an almost instant copy of virtually any kind of document. Facsimile transmission of data – commonly known as *fax* transmission – requires only that those interested should subscribe to the public fax service. Put simply, a fax terminal is a combination of a photocopier and a telephone.

You simply dial up the number of the person whom you wish to have a copy of your document, place the document on your machine, and within a few seconds your friend will have a reasonably good quality copy!

If you are not a subscriber to the fax system, you may avail yourself of a public service run by the Post Office. Most main Post Offices have a fax machine from which, in return for the current fee, you may transmit your documents to the main Post Office nearest to your friend or client. A telephone call will then alert them to collect the fax copy documents.

As facsimile transmission of data involves making a hard copy, you may be sure that copyrights are involved in some shape or form, and indeed it is considered that a fax machine is just another form of photocopier. So, in general, all of the photocopying rules outlined above apply equally to fax users.

Illegal use of photocopiers

It is suspected that many cases of copyright infringement, by photocopying and other means, are settled out of court. However, with evasion of the copyright laws being taken increasingly seriously, it's a useful exercise to remind ourselves of some of the more prominent cases over recent years.

One of the most publicised copyright cases was that of the Music Publishers' Association *versus* Oakham School, Leicestershire, in 1981. It had come to light that the school had been making copies of various songs and other musical scores owned by members of the Music Publishers' Association. The Association took legal action on behalf of its members. The school was found guilty, and was fined £4250 which included £400 exemplary damages. In addition, of course, the school had to pay its own costs.

The Music Publishers' Association had, a year prior to the Oakham School case, taken to court the Wolverhampton Education Authority for matters pertaining to illicit copies of various works owned by Association members. Upon being found guilty, the defendants were fined £1300. They were also ordered to pay costs amounting to over £2000 and they, too, had their own costs to pay on top of all this.

While Oakham School were busy defending themselves in the UK court in 1981, three British publishers joined forces against a college in Virginia in the United States of America. The publishers in question were Oxford University Press, Theodore Presser Company, and Novello & Co Ltd. The publishers alleged that the American college had indulged in wilful infringement of copyright, and stated quite categorically that copyrights owned by them had been violated through being photocopied without any permission. Upon being found guilty, the defendants agreed to pay all damages and attorneys' fees, as well as giving an undertaking that they would refrain from any further such photocopying.

More recently in America, a ruling from the Federal Court at Manhattan provided the plaintiffs with an historical victory as well as setting an intriguing new precedent as far as American copyright cases are concerned. The plaintiffs were a group of publishers that had got together to take a joint action. These consisted of the American Geophysical Union, the Elsevier Science Publishing Company, Pergamon Press Ltd, Springer-Verlag Gmbh, John Wiley & Sons and Wiley Heyden Ltd. These individual publishers were supported by the Association of American Publishers acting both on their own behalf as well as on behalf of approximately 600 other publishing concerns. Jointly, these plaintiffs alleged that the defendants, Texaco Inc., regularly made photocopies of articles published in such periodicals as scientific and technical journals. It was known that Texaco made nominal payments to the American Copyright Clearance Center, but the plaintiffs argued that these payments were strictly nominal and completely unacceptable.

Texaco's lawyer attempted to have the action dismissed on the grounds that the plaintiffs had "failed to comply with certain provisions of the Copyright Act". Further, Texaco had also requested the court not to proceed with a hearing because of the 'class' of the publishers concerned.

These petitions were debated, and the plaintiffs claimed that as the alleged photocopying was undertaken internally by Texaco employees, they could not actually specify particular details of works that were being copied contrary to the appropriate legislation. They also suggested that the copying from journals put out by their 'class' of publishing houses was, in itself, an appropriate argument for proceeding with the case. As a result of the debate, on 19 June 1986 the US District Court ruled that the plaintiffs were entitled to proceed with their action, and to do so on a 'class' basis! The Court obviously recognized that copyright owners have the right to take legal action against those who photocopy their works without having prior permission.

Earlier in 1986, two local authorities had been found guilty of violating the Copyright Act. In England, Manchester City Council had been undertaking illegal 'educational photocopying' for which they had to pay £50 000 damages and £25 000 costs (in addition to their own costs). In Scotland, Strathclyde County Council had been the defendants in several cases of copyright infringement and they had to find £1200 legal costs plus £250 damages (again, their own costs would have been additional to these sums).

It will be readily appreciated that this handful of examples of copyright cases have been selected from those that have been afforded considerable publicity. It is believed that many cases do not reach the attention of the media, and minor cases, if reported at all, will be found published only in the local press. It is further reckoned that many, many cases are settled out of court when copyright owners discover an infringement of one or more of their works, and take up the matter directly with the guilty party. In such instances, the offender very often accepts the situation and pays the copyright owner whatever sum is agreed between the two parties. It is probable that individual infringers of copyright generally settle their cases out of court in view of the fact that one rarely learns of an individual person having to provide some sort of defence or explanation at the bar.

3
The written word

Most aspiring authors look forward to the day when they will see their names in print. Countless typewriter ribbons are worn bare every month, as the hardest triers in this field plod on regardless through reams of paper. (The more successful ones, of course, avoid the ribbons – and even possibly the paper – by using word processors). It's a fact of publishing life that thousands of manuscripts are written, but only a small percentage ever become books.

If this hasn't put you off, and you are aware that another fact of publishing life is that very, very few authors earn enough shekels to make more than the smallest dent in their mortgage repayment, then, presumably, you'd like to know exactly what to do with your exceptional manuscript.

It doesn't have to be a book, of course. It may be a slim collection of poems that could well be included in a larger anthology; or an essay that might fit the bill for a magazine article. Whatever your work is, the general procedures are the same, and we will assume it's a book for the purpose of this chapter.

First things first

The very first thing *must* be your claim to the copyright in your work. If you dictate your work onto tape for typing out at some later date, perhaps by a secretary that you employ specially, or by an agency, always start by clearly stating that what follows is your copyright. If you write it out, then use the international copyright symbol © on the first page, followed by your name and the date, usually abbreviated to just the year.

When your work is accepted for inclusion in the programme of a commercial publishing house, it is usual for the publisher to ask you to sign a publishing contract. One of the most important clauses in this contract requires you to warrant that the work is your own original work and is therefore your copyright. The publisher may offer to buy your copyright. If you sell, then you would need the publisher's written permission to use your own work in the future.

Many publishers will also ask you to agree that they may publish

"Make sure the author is suitably identified on the cover."

your work in all countries of the world, and that they may negotiate such things as magazine serial rights, television, video and film rights, and so on. In other words, the publisher wants you to agree that they should be the agent for your work. This is a sensible attitude, because publishers are often in the position of being able to negotiate the best possible terms on your behalf. Whatever payments the publisher receives in respect of any of these rights is shared on an agreed basis with you, the author. Charles Clark, who is currently Chairman of the International Publishers' Association's Copyright Committee, has collected together a number of precedents of various publishing agreements for the serious seeker after more detailed information: *Publishing Agreements*, published by George Allen & Unwin Ltd.

Whatever publisher you have an agreement with, under the Copyright, Designs and Patents Act 1988, you do have the *moral right* to have your name published as the legitimate author of the book. This moral right applies to all manner of intellectual property excluding certain works such as dictionaries, yearbooks and encyclopedias. Of course, any author can waive this moral right, which he should do in writing. See the further information on moral rights on page 17 You are recommended to make sure the author is suitably identified on the cover of your book. Similar rights apply to illustrators.

Subsidiary rights

There are a great many other 'rights' that publishers like to negotiate on behalf of their authors, and it's well worth us taking just a brief look at some of the more common ones.

Mechanical rights

These are the rights conferred on copyright material that is committed to some form of audio recording. In these enlightened times, more and more volumes of print have the additional potential to become 'talking books' by being made available on audio tape cassettes which can be played in the car just as easily as at home. Should your work ever merit release in this way, your reward will be the royalty that you earn from the mechanical right.

Paperback rights

When books are first published in a hardback format, some other publisher may perceive that there is commercial potential in issuing a paperback edition. The original publisher of the casebound edition could sell to the second publisher the 'right' to issue the work in a paperbound format. The author then enjoys the benefit of royalties on both editions of his work.

Foreign rights

Once your potential bestseller has been published by a British publisher, that publisher will distribute the book, to the best of his ability, to outlets throughout the British Isles. It may be that your publisher also has the advantage of a distribution network in selected other countries such as those which constitute the European Economic Community. Nevertheless, distribution to these other countries will still be only of the English language edition.

Foreign rights can be divided into two distinct classifications. *Foreign distribution rights* are negotiated by the original British publisher with a local publisher in a particular foreign territory who will import stocks of the book for distribution within his territory to customers who are on the lookout for books printed in English.

Your publisher could also negotiate the *translation rights* with a publisher in another country to undertake a translation of your work and publish the resulting foreign edition, distributing it either in his own country or within a defined territory. In this case, you would earn royalties derived from this foreign language edition.

Film and video rights

These rights are rather similar to mechanical rights (see above), except that instead of receiving your royalty based on sales of an audio recording, your royalties would be in respect of a video recording or a cinematograph film.

However, it is usual, when a book is converted into a film or videogram, for many adaptations to be made in order to produce a realistic screen version. When this happens, the term used in your contract might be something like *dramatization right* or *documentary right*. As such adaptations of an original story are common in broadcasting, these terms should be borne in mind when considering broadcast rights (especially television, cable diffusion, etc.). Not surprisingly, perhaps, some astute negotiators use the universal description *film, television and allied rights*.

Broadcast rights

As the name implies, broadcast rights come into operation when part, or all, of your book is read on a radio broadcast or in a television programme, or if a film or video has been made based on your volume, and transmitted by television. Broadcast rights include transmission on a diffusion system, cable system or satellite system. In Britain, fees payable in respect of such broadcasting are often negotiated between the Publishers Association (acting on behalf of all its members) and bodies such as the British Broadcasting Corporation and the Independent Broadcasting Authority. However, publishers and other copyright owners are still free to undertake their own negotiations with those broadcasters who are not affiliated to either the BBC or IBA, such as local community broadcasting companies.

Non-commercial rights

These rights relate to items produced by certain organizations in order to help those within our community who are disabled. The Copyright Act does not prohibit copyright owners or their agents from making a charge to use their works, but over the years a tradition has built up whereby permission is normally given free of any charge, on condition that the customary full acknowledgement is granted to the author and publisher. As the name implies, the items that are produced will *not* be used or sold for commercial purposes or financial gain.

The most common example is the adaptation of copyright books for the visually handicapped and certified blind. Organizations of a charitable status, such as the Royal National Institute for the Blind (RNIB), the National Library for the Blind in the United Kingdom (NLBUK) and the Torch Trust for the Blind (TTB) like to reproduce a limited number of copies of either complete books or parts of books, in formats that our sightless friends can read. The books may be issued in Braille, or an audio cassette may be produced. For the visually handicapped, printed books are sometimes produced, using a very large, clear type.

Other disabled people requiring assistance are those who are physically unable, for one reason or another, to hold or read books produced in the usual way. These folk often rely on audio tapes for their 'reading' enjoyment.

Virtually all hospitals boast their own hospital radio broadcasting service, run on a charitable basis by volunteers, and supported by wellwishers such as a league of friends. It is debatable whether or not these hospital radio broadcasters should seek free use of copyright material to enhance their services. It is believed that some copyright owners do give free consent, whereas others charge a nominal fee. In either case, most hospital radio stations like to read a chapter of a book each day, as a series of broadcasts, and some like to read short stories for children or poems in order to cheer up some of the younger patients. In all cases, it is essential to insist that the usual acknowledgement to the author and publisher is given during each transmission. Some authors and publishers take the view that hospital radio could be a form of cheap advertising, because if patients are attracted to a particular work, they may go out and buy it, once they are convalescent.

Serial rights

If a newspaper or magazine wished to publish your book as a series of articles, perhaps a chapter at a time over a period of weeks or months, they would need to negotiate with your publisher for the serial rights. Sometimes, a publisher's marketing department might approach the editors of selected periodicals in an endeavour to sell the serial rights prior to the publication of the actual book. Such a move would be made because the publisher anticipates that selling the serial rights would produce publicity for your book that might otherwise not be available.

Some authors used to believe that publishing their work in serial form could have an adverse effect on the general book sales. However, it has now been shown that such sales are more likely to increase, so that authors tend to try and encourage their publishers to capitalize on the serial rights!

Subsidiary rights

All of the above-mentioned rights, along with any other forms of exploitation of your work negotiated on your behalf by your publisher, are collectively known as the *subsidiary rights*. Remember, even if you have only a small extract of your work published or utilized by another commercial body, but handled by your publisher, you should receive a royalty payment in respect of the appropriate subsidiary right.

In return for negotiating on your behalf, your publisher retains a percentage of the royalty to help with his own expenses. Whatever commission your publisher is entitled to ought to be included in your agreement.

The 'world territories' usually defined for subsidiary rights are Africa, Antarctica, Asia, Central America, Europe, Oceania, North America and Canada, and South America. However, it is important to bear in mind that any country (indeed, even part of a country) could be a territory negotiated for any particular right.

Other subsidiary rights

Apart from the various subsidiary rights mentioned in the preceding few paragraphs, there are certain others, some or all of which might be named in your contract with your publisher. It goes without saying, perhaps, that some publishers include in their contracts a cleverly worded phrase that is designed to cover all such rights, e.g.

"We, Gettem and Sellem (Publishers) Plc, reserve the right to negotiate on behalf of the aforementioned author, in respect of the aforementioned work, any other edition, or abstract, or merchandising, or any other subsidiary benefit that may be deemed to accrue whilst our edition remains in print".

Additional subsidiary rights that you may encounter are:

Book club rights

These are the rights that a book club can purchase, to publish either exclusively or non-exclusively their own special book club edition of your tome.

Condensed book rights

The buyer of these rights is authorized to publish a shortened version of your book. Sometimes a book club might negotiate with your publisher to issue a book club edition of your work in a condensed format.

Anthology rights

These are particularly common with collections of verse and/or small pieces of prose. The buyer's intention is to issue your work, alongside many others, in an anthology. It is possible to negotiate to use an extract from, say, a novel in an anthology.

Strip cartoon rights

If your work happens to feature a main character, or characters, that could possibly form a basis for a series of strip cartoons, then one day you could be receiving royalties earned from the strip cartoon rights. Newspapers and comics are the most common buyers of such rights, though nowadays they usually prefer to create their own characters.

Merchandising rights

If your main character and story setting catch on, your enterprising publisher may well negotiate the sale of merchandising rights on your behalf. The buyer of merchandising rights acquires the use of your created characters to assist in merchandising his own products – perfumes, soaps, toys, stationery, games, etc. As an example, Raymond Briggs wrote an original story entitled *The Snowman*. This proved to be popular, and the book sells well. Many entrepreneurs saw the business potential of the character. A videogram was produced (video right), the video has been transmitted on television (television broadcasting right), and numerous goods are on sale, relying on the 'snowman' popularity for sales, including bubble bath, soap, toys and stationery items (merchandising right).

Merchandising rights in children's book characters are becoming increasingly valuable as the food industry seeks them (e.g. Mr Men cheese spread or Munch Bunch yoghurts).

Biblical copyright

Bookselling statistics indicate that the bible is still the world's bestselling book, and therefore it deserves a special mention. It is not necessarily immediately apparent that, although the *Authorized Version* is out of copyright, a number of versions do enjoy copyright protection.

Each time the bible is published in a new translation or version, recent examples of which are the *New English Bible*, the *Good News Bible* and the *New International Version*, a new copyright is created, which is the property of the translator(s) or those persons responsible for creating the new 'version'. There is also a typographical copyright involved, which belongs to the publisher, and newly produced editions even of the *Authorized Version* would be covered by this.

So, if you want to reproduce part of the bible, the normal rules apply, namely that you should seek permission from the publisher in respect of any copyright edition or, for photocopying, any edition produced within the past 25 years.

Public Lending Right

Unlike subsidiary rights, Public Lending Right is *not* a potential earner negotiated on your behalf by your publisher. It is a fee paid to authors and illustrators whose books are frequently borrowed by members of the public through their local public library service. For some years, the Society of Authors, along with some other sympathetic bodies, campaigned for such a fee to be paid, taking the view that authors lost out when their books were borrowed rather than purchased.

Their labours eventually bore fruit when the Public Lending Right payment scheme was introduced in July 1983. It took an Act of Parliament to bring it into effect: the rather short, but obligatory,

Public Lending Right Act of 1979, followed by the Public Lending Right Scheme 1982, and various amendment orders.

Under the Public Lending Right system, payment is made annually from public funds allocated by Parliament. The actual sum to be allocated each year is usually announced by the Arts Minister, the sum for 1988/89 being £3.5 million (representing 1.45 pence per loan), increasing in 1991/92 to £4.25 million.

Although public libraries are known to lend out items other than books (such as audio cassettes, gramophone records and, more recently, videograms), the 1979 act expressly restricts payment of the Public Lending Right to authors and illustrators of *books*. Further, the act stresses that payments are to be made to the account of the author (or authors and/or illustrators) from the outset, irrespective of whether or not the first owner of the copyright is the author. However, the right may be assigned by the author, in the same way that he may assign his copyright in the original work.

Public Lending Right is payable during the term of the original copyright (i.e. until 50 years from the end of the calendar year in which the author dies).

With the hundreds of thousands of books available on loan from public libraries throughout the United Kingdom, the sums earned through the Public Lending Right legislation are not paid automatically. If an author wishes to be included in the scheme, he must indicate this by joining the Public Lending Right Register. No charge is levied to authors wishing to have their names added to the register; all that is necessary is to complete an application form acquired from the Public Lending Right Registrar (see Appendix 2 for the address).

As might be expected, there are a few conditions applicable to the PLR scheme. Writers, illustrators (including photographers), translators, compilers, editors and revisers are all classified as authors or co-authors, so long as they have each contributed a substantial amount of effort to a published book, and that their names appear on the title page. Such authors must be resident in the United Kingdom or the Federal Republic of Germany. Books themselves qualify only if there are *no more than* three named writers or illustrators.

Unlike the majority of 'rights' payments, authors' receipts from the Public Lending Right fund are *not* royalties. They are payments made from a public fund and, as such, are outside of the scope of Value Added Tax. Some authors and illustrators are self-employed and declare their royalties on their VAT return form. PLR payments should not be declared on the VAT document although, of course, they should still be included as income on Income Tax returns.

Vanity publishers

Publishers reward you for hard work in researching and writing a book by either buying your copyright for a mutually agreed sum, or by paying you a royalty on each copy of your book that they are able to sell. However, you may come across a publisher that offers to publish your work if *you* pay *them*. These concerns are known as 'vanity publishers' and really act as a sort of printing and publishing service. Most of them require you to take a large stock of your own book, so that in effect you have probably simply paid a firm to produce a quantity of books, the majority of which you then have to distribute yourself through any means you think fit. Rather than set something up with a vanity publisher, you may prefer to organize the entire project yourself, and become the publisher as well as the author.

Note that, if you do use a vanity publisher, they will retain the copyright in the typographical arrangement because their name is used as the publisher or imprint. You should, however, ensure that you retain copyright in the text.

Adaptations

As the making of an adaptation of a literary, dramatic or musical work without prior permission of the copyright owner is an infringement of copyright, remember that if you are involved in adapting a work, perhaps in order to stage an amateur theatrical production, you should check to see if the work is in copyright and, if it is, obtain the necessary permission.

A special consideration applies to J M Barrie's *Peter Pan*, the copyright of which expired on 31 December 1987. See page 105.

Copyright of titles and characters

When writing a book, comic strip, or even a short magazine article, the author may create a character out of his imagination. Enid Blyton created *Noddy* and *Big Ears*, Captain W E Johns invented *Biggles*, and Sir Arthur Conan Doyle really did create *Sherlock Holmes*! However, do not be misled into thinking that, as you have given birth to an original, fictitious character, your new baby is protected by copyright legislation. Our UK rules provide that there is *no* claim to copyright in such characters. Copyright subsists only in the work in which your character is featured.

Take, for example, Sherlock Holmes. Some years ago, a writer produced some 'new' stories in which our hero always got his man. He was found not guilty of copyright infringement, having produced fresh and original stories.

More recently, the journal *Teachers' Weekly* featured a comic strip story of Noddy and Big Ears. Again, no breach of copyright has taken place, because even though the story was not written by Enid Blyton, *Noddy in No-Man's Land* consisted of original text.

Likewise, there is no legal basis for copyright in book titles, or the name of a drama, or piece of poetry, or even the title of a work of art. It's not recommended to use another author's title simply because you're having difficulty coming up with an original one of your own. For one thing, the other chap's book might not be as good as yours and therefore have a poor reputation amongst booksellers. They might associate low sales with that title, and the end result could be detrimental to your potential bestseller! On the other hand, if you crib somebody else's title because *theirs* is a bestseller, you may be accused of jumping on a literary bandwaggon, and perhaps even lay yourself open to charges of misrepresentation.

Some duplication of titles is inevitable. It has been known for a publishing house to have two completely separate books in their list with either identical, or extemely similar, titles! Think what confusion that can bring!

With regard to names and characters it is, of course, possible to register a name as a trade mark (see page 98). However, as the description implies, to do so you would have to be using that particular name as a trading device. Further, it would have to be written in a unique way that would always be reproduced on the wares that you are marketing. For example, the name *Oxo* is a registered trade mark of Brooke Bond Oxo Ltd, and refers to that company's stock cube products. The name *Oxo* is reproduced in an original graphic style and, as such, appears on all the relevant products, packaging, advertising, and so on. So, it is highly improbable that you would be able to register as a trade mark the name of your new character unless it is written in a particular graphic style and merchandising rights are involved.

Legal deposit

Under various pieces of copyright legislation within the UK, complimentary copies of all publications *must* be supplied to certain libraries, designated as official copyright libraries. The main one is the British Library, which has a legal requirement to maintain a national archive of published works. Publications have to be supplied within one month of publication, and the earlier the better, so it is recommended that you supply your official copyright library copies just as soon as you have received stocks from your printer.

This requirement is a consequence of the British Library Act of 1972, which lays down that if a publisher fails to comply with his legal obligations, he may be convicted. In this case, the publisher's obligations are to furnish the British Library (Copyright Receipt Office address in Appendix 2) with a copy of the best edition of the book that is being made available to the public. In practice, many publishers supply one copy of each edition.

The law uses the word *book* to include "every part or division of a book, pamphlet, sheet of letterpress, sheet of music, map, plan, chart or table separately published".

The Library always issues receipts to publishers, so you will know that your book has been safely delivered. Incidentally, the British Library does *not* accept unpublished manuscripts or typescripts, etc., *nor* does the supply of a book to the British Library, or to any other official copyright library, serve as a registration of, or proof of ownership of, any copyrights.

In addition to the British Library, there are five other official copyright libraries within Britain and Ireland to which you must supply complimentary copies of your work either voluntarily or when requested. These are the Bodleian Library Oxford, the University Library Cambridge, the National Library of Scotland, the Library of Trinity College Dublin, and the National Library of Wales. The requirement to supply British books to the Library of Trinity College, Dublin, comes about through copyright legislation applicable to books published and/or distributed in the UK. The Irish Copyright Act of 1963 provides that the publisher of any book first published in the Republic of Ireland shall be required to deliver a complimentary copy to the British Library, so a reciprocal arrangement exists.

Fortunately, some years ago, these various copyright libraries got together to appoint an agent to collect all publications on their behalf. So all you need to do is to wrap up one parcel, containing five copies of your potential bestseller, and address the package to Mr A T Smail in London (address in Appendix 2). Mr Smail will furnish you with a receipt, so that you'll know he received all five copies in good condition, and he then takes the responsibility for ensuring that each of the libraries in question receives a copy of your book.

In the case of serials, i.e. periodicals, journals, newspapers, annuals, etc., one copy of each issue is required to be deposited at each of the six copyright libraries.

Exempt from the deposit regulations are certain categories of works that it would seem ludicrous for these various libraries to file. However, publishers are obliged to supply complimentary copies of these so-called *exempt* works to any such library making a written demand. The exempt works are trade advertisements, timetables prepared for local use (e.g. bus or train timetables), calendars, blank forms (e.g. receipts, petty cash vouchers, order forms), wall sheets printed with alphabets, religious texts, optical texts, elementary instruction matter, etc.

Your own society

Should you become an author, you may like to consider joining the *Society of Authors*. This organization, whose address you will find in Appendix 2, was founded in 1884 to promote the interest of authors and to defend their rights. The Society advises its members on matters pertinent to writing, including matters concerning copyright.

Book Piracy

In recent times, the media has given attention to such topics of copyright theft as video piracy and computer software piracy, but one doesn't seem to hear so much about book piracy. Nevertheless, book piracy is a real problem, and needs to be curbed as much as any other form of copyright pirating.

Any piece of intellectual property and innovation that has ever been published in any medium has only acquired its commercial form through the painstaking planning, marketing and, above all, investment of its publishers.

In the case of a book, the author may have spent many years in costly research before the publishers pitched in their financial contribution to get the production under way. Likewise, with sheet music and musical scores, the composers may well have spent years getting their work perfected.

Some books are now published, not only as a printed paper version, but also on audio cassettes and records. These 'talking books' are probably read and recorded at a studio. As with the printed editions, the publishers have to invest hundreds of pounds in studio time and mastering, producing appropriate packaging and advertising, and distribution.

Sometimes a publisher considers that a bestselling title warrants the additional investment needed to issue it in another format, such as on video cassette. For instance, the *Teddy Horsley* children's stories published by Collins have been released on a couple of videos by Wheaton Publishing.

Publishers of scientific, technical and medical reference books or legal works often add the texts onto a computer database for instant retrieval or onto a CD-ROM disk for reference in bookshops or libraries. With all this capital investment, it is no wonder that it has been said that international piracy is the biggest threat to the British producers of copyright material!

Piracy, or the production of an illicit copy of anything, can only be described as outright theft. Publishers who have invested large sums of money in their works need to sell their productions on a commercial scale in order to (a) get back their investment, (b) pay royalties to their authors and illustrators, and (c) obtain a return on their investment, in the form of profit, to pay their staff and ensure that there is some money in the kitty to invest in future production.

Whenever an infringing copy of a work is produced and distributed, everybody loses out. In 1984/85 it was estimated that sales abroad of pirate books and other wares, such as tapes, videos and computer software cost the UK book publishing and music industries something like £158 million in lost income from just eight selected publishing territories: Singapore, Malaysia, Taiwan, Korea, Indonesia, Pakistan, Saudi Arabia and Nigeria. So just try to imagine what the cost of total worldwide piracy of UK products must be like! Fortunately for the sanity of honest publishers, trade and other organizations are doing their utmost to persuade these and other countries to conform to sensible guidelines. The good news is that both Singapore and Korea introduced their own copyright legislation during 1987.

A similar story seems to be emerging in the United States of America. The US Intellectual Property Alliance has estimated that copyright piracy in just ten selected publishing areas costs the American economy something like $1.3 billion annually.

Although there appear to be no firm statistics available pertinent to book piracy specifically, the 1988 EEC *Copyright Green Paper* mentioned that in 1983 piracy of books outside of the European Community was estimated to be costing publishers something in the region of $1 billion annually. The Green Paper considers that this figure was probably still valid five years later in 1988.

Another consequence of copyright piracy is lost jobs. Lost sales of the magnitude of these mentioned above effectively mean lost markets, which in turn lead to reduced employment.

Apart from the loss to publishers, the British economy is another party that comes off badly as a result of copyright theft. Where bootleg copies of materials are sold, the proceeds are pocketed by the pirates. In honest dealings, sales of books make a positive contribution to the government treasury.

Legal action

As has been reported in the press from time to time, UK publishers do take steps to defend their copyright works from exploitation. Book publishers and recording companies have taken action against offenders of copyright laws. They have initiated both criminal and civil actions, with the result that the courts have seized infringing copies of books and recordings.

It is generally believed that the amount of copyright piracy that is actually known to be going on is only the tip of the iceberg. Consequently, copyright owners and their agents are constantly pressing for stiffer penalties to be imposed upon those found to be guilty. Remedies for the infringement of various rights therefore form an important contribution to current legislation.

Acknowledgement

Some of the facts and figures quoted above are from *International Piracy: the threat to the British copyright industries*, available from the Publishers Association.

A recent case

At the end of 1988, Macmillan announced that they had reached an out-of-court settlement in connection with book piracy that had taken place in Korea. It concerned their *The New Palgrave: A Dictionary of Economics*, which is published in no less than four substantial volumes, and took about five years to compile. More than 900 people were employed on the project, including 13 winners of the Nobel Prize, and Macmillan's investment was said to be $1.5 million.

The New Palgrave was published in November 1987. Ironically this was barely one month after Korea's accession to the Universal Copyright Convention, because Macmillan alleged that something in the region of 200 sets of the volumes had been manufactured illegally in Seoul by the time that Korea received supplies of the honest edition. It appears that the pirate copies had been produced by a Mr Park Ki Bong of the Bibong Publishing Company, Seoul.

Interestingly enough, Macmillan accepted what can only be described as a modest financial payment of £5000 (the work retails at £425 per set in the United Kingdom) on condition that they received a public apology printed in a Korean tabloid. Such an apology appeared in the *Korea Herald*: "We [Bibong Publishing Company] sincerely apologize for inflicting damage on Macmillan Publishers Ltd, the copyright holder, and Pan Korea Book Corporation, the licensed distributor of the above stated publication [*The New Palgrave*], by illegally reproducing and selling unauthorized copies in violation of the Korean Copyright Law. We further agree that no unauthorized reproduction and sales activities shall be carried out by us in the future".

Although Macmillan, it could be argued, probably gained some useful publicity from this press statement, they should be commended for their insistence upon it. Such a public statement makes it abundantly clear that copyright owners take a dim view of piracy, and hopefully this serves to deter any would-be pirates. The outcome of this settlement is, surely, that Macmillan have effectively supported *all* copyright holders, not just themselves.

Towards a European policy

Debating a European policy statement for books, the British Publishers Association issued an important press release in December 1986 which included the following:

Copyright, the protection of intellectual property, is the foundation stone of authorship and publishing. It is a stimulus to creativity rather than a barrier. It receives the protection of international conventions and national laws, to enable authors to earn material rewards and recognition for their work, and to protect its integrity, by giving them the exclusive right to control reproduction, to enable creative works to be made available on the market through effective licensing arrangements, and also, most importantly, to secure the public interest that works of the mind should be widely disseminated. Copyright meets these basic requirements. It is also essential to protect and encourage the translation of creative works into other languages.

The European Publishers Group (GELC) working closely with its principal body, the International Publishers Association, and with the International Group of Scientific, Technical and Medical Publishers, STM (also affiliated to the IPA) accords the highest importance to the protection of copyright.

Effective operation of copyright requires the Community and the member states to:

take effective action against unauthorized reproduction of works for sale (piracy). This requires effective detection procedures, discouragement of trading agreements with countries not providing adequate copyright protection, and severe penalties for piracy in national law. These activities should be part of the accepted programme of the Commission;

bring about sensible harmonization of copyright laws through the Community to avoid discriminatory conditions in different member states. The European Publishers Group (GELC) is most interested in and concerned about this crucial development of EEC law, and stresses the need for consultation with the publishing industry;

recognize that unauthorized reproduction through computers and through reprography, both in institutions and commercial organizations and by private copying, destroys the viability of publishing and prospects of return on the investment involved, and is contrary to international conventions;

give support to sensible collective licensing systems to permit reasonable copying by reprographic means without prior permission, but with an adequate and fair return to the copyright owner, based on the use made of works, on a similar basis throughout the Community – providing better safeguards against illegal copying;

afford adequate protection to electronic publishing rights, particularly through protection of works loaded into computers for storage and reproduction, and to computer programs, databases and output;

avoid measures such as Domaine Public Payant, imposing a tax on works in the public domain;

protect national and regional cultures, and to recognize the need for books in different languages to be distributed in the different language areas of the Community, by permitting exclusive publishing and distribution rights in copyright in the different language areas, so enabling viable publishing to take place;

put continued pressure on the governing bodies of the international copyright organizations (WIPO and UNESCO) to recognize and assert the importance of the viability of authors and publishers in making works of the mind available;

recognize that publishers play an essential role in the dissemination of works of the mind, and that they can only fulfil this role if they are able to earn an adequate and fair return on their skills and investments, through a sufficient interest in the copyright in the works they publish, and by good contractual practices.

In 1988, the EEC published their *Green Paper* on copyright, a discussion document which looks forward towards harmonization of copyright legislation within the European Community.

4
Sound recordings _____

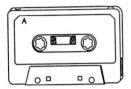

Once an intellectual work has been captured onto magnetic tape, it is automatically in copyright. It is becoming common practice for people committing their masterpieces to tape to put the Universal Copyright Convention symbol © on the tape box and/or label, although this is not necessary if copyright is required to be restricted, for some reason, to those countries that are signatories to the Berne Convention.

Some songwriters and composers of other musical works put their efforts initially onto tape, to be transcribed into 'written down' music at some later date. It is a common misconception that works are not in copyright until they are written down. This is not so. Your copyright exists the moment you record a passage. Further, if you compose a work that you commit to tape for somebody else to transcribe into a written form, the copyright is still your property. The person employed to undertake the transcription work has no claim to any copyright in that work (unless, of course, you choose to assign your copyright to them).

Copyright law, interestingly enough, provides that there is an entirely separate right in the recording, as distinct from the right in the original written down work. So, if you have written a song and Groovy Recordings have recorded it onto tape, you may sign a contract with Groovy Recordings giving them the authority to publish a recording while you retain the copyright of the original work. You then own the copyright in the *original work*, but Groovy

Recordings own the copyright of the *recording*.

The rules remain the same irrespective of what form the recording finally takes, the most common end products being audio cassettes, audio records, compact disc and digital audio tape products. Advancing digital technology will doubtless produce yet more media for sound recordings. Meanwhile we must not overlook current products that contain an audio track, usually referred to as the *soundtrack*, such as videograms and cinematograph films.

Some time ago, I found myself involved in a situation where somebody who was an amateur photographer put together a sequence of slide transparencies, complete with a taped commentary. A couple of the photographs were not his originals, but he was careful to obtain permission from the appropriate source to include them in his programme, which was to be shown to a youth club. The taped commentary included snippets of an interview and, as Murphy's Law would have it, one of the interviewees happened to be one of the club's youth workers. And – yes, you've guessed correctly – my acquaintance had been so involved in the pictures side of his presentation that he'd quite overlooked that separate and distinct copyright applied to the audio back-up. Fortunately, in this instance, the youth worker had no objections. But the outcome could have been rather less than pleasant.

Suppose that you commission a recording studio to make a tape of a song you have composed. Perhaps you simply want just one tape to play to a publisher, demonstrating how you feel the work should sound. Or you might want a few cassettes to give to your acquaintances to help fill their Christmas stockings, and provide you with the advantage of a bit of publicity. Whatever the circumstances, the fact is that you have *commissioned* the studio to undertake the recording work on your behalf. Once you have paid the studio company's invoice, and taken delivery of your master tape, the copyright in *that recording* is yours. Not, as some people have mistakenly thought, the property of the recording company! Similarly, if you sign up with a record publisher, the chances are that they will commission a studio to record your work. In this instance, of course, your publishers will meet the cost, and *they* will own the recording right.

Subsequent recordings

Subsequent recordings are additional, but none-the-less original, recordings of works already recorded. Suppose, for example, that Bandwidth Records have recorded your song using studio musicians to accompany the voice of Fantasia Skyenote. At some later date,

Pyramid Music decide to issue a recording using last year's Eurovision Song Contest winner, backed by that irresistible group, The Mummies. Pyramid Music's recording would be a subsequent recording.

In recent years both commercial and private recording companies have been releasing audio recordings under a clause in the 1956 Copyright Act, commonly known as the *Statutory Recording Licence*. The Statutory Recording Licence was in fact originally conceived as part of the 1911 Copyright Act, probably to assist the recording industry which was a 'new technology' in those days. Basically this licence meant that, once a recording of a work had been produced for the purposes of retail sale, to which the copyright owner of that work would have agreed, any other organization enjoyed the automatic right to produce its own original recordings of that work. Those who issued such subsequent recordings had to comply with the condition that they paid the copyright owner a royalty on all copies sold, the royalty being 6¼ per cent of the recommended retail price excluding tax. In other words, under the 1956 Statutory Recording Licence, once you had authorized the making of a sound recording of your work for retail sale, you lost any control over the making of any further original recordings.

The good news for copyright owners, who may well have been concerned lest they were being exploited by disreputable recording companies failing to pay the appropriate royalties, is that the 1988 Act has repealed the Statutory Recording Licence. In future, anyone wishing to record a work, irrespective of whether or not it has previously been recorded, must first obtain full permission from the owner of the copyright in that work.

Inevitably, there must be a short transitional period while subsequent recordings that have already been legitimately produced under the old Statutory Recording Licence continue to be sold. It is recognized that various queries or disputes may well arise and the Copyright Tribunal is therefore empowered to settle such disputes.

Private circulation recordings

Many amateur groups – operatic groups, choirs, etc. – like to record their events and produce copies, usually on audio cassettes, for circulation among their members and friends. In situations where the copyright(s) of the work(s) to be recorded are owned by members of the Mechanical-Copyright Protection Society, it is a simple matter to obtain a licence permitting such a recording. This is because MCPS, on behalf if its members, offer what is known as a *Miscel-*

laneous *Recording Licence*. Issue of this licence is conditonal upon the recordings not being sold by retailing them in the normal manner through shops or mail order. MCPS will advise you if any works do not belong to any of its members. At the time of writing, the licence fee is £5.75 including VAT to permit up to 50 copies of the recording to be produced, and double that sum for up to 100 copies.

Commercial importing

Under copyright legislation, licences are needed from the UK copyright owners of both the work recorded and the sound recording prior to any commercial importation into the UK of such items manufactured outside of the European Economic Community (EEC).

In order to simplify the administration of such import licences for music recordings, MCPS (representing the majority of music copyright holders) and the British Phonographic Industry (representing the sound recording copyright holders) have got together to grant one licence to cover both copyrights *as held by their members*. Separate import licences must be obtained from non-members of these organizations.

Application forms to obtain both the *Miscellaneous Recording Licence* and the *Commercial Import Licence for Audio Recordings* are available direct from the Mechanical-Copyright Protection Society (the address is given in Appendix 2).

Re-recording of records and tapes

Legally, it is prohibited for anyone to re-record, without prior permission, any record or tape, including the soundtrack of a vision tape or film, or similar product. This applies even when the recording is intended only for private use in one's own home! And when seeking permission to re-record an item, remember that there is nearly always a minimum of two permissions required: one from the copyright owner of the work recorded, the other from the copyright owner of the published work, usually the record company. There could be additional music copyrights which would technically require permission, for example, there could well be copyright in the arrangement, and it might also be necessary to have permission from the publishing company if this happens to be different from the recording company.

Here is an example of the last point. A commercial recording of a musical entitled *Greater than Gold* is recorded on the Riverbank label. If you wished to re-record part, or all, of this musical, you would need authorization from Riverbank. However, it happens that in this instance the work is actually published by the National Christian Education Council, so you would also need permission from them. All this would no doubt be made clear when you applied to either company for permission!

Getting permission to re-record an audio production is sometimes far from being a simple matter. Some 20 years ago, if my memory serves me well, a school operatic society proposed to stage a production of *Trial by Jury*, the popular comical dramatic cantata in one act from the Savoy Operas. The libretto had been written by W S Gilbert and the music composed by Arthur Sullivan. The complete work had been recorded by a well-known gramophone record publishing company, and the school, having purchased a copy of the record, wanted to dub individual songs onto tape to assist their soloists and others in learning their parts.

The words, in fact, were out of copyright, Mr Gilbert having died more than 50 years previously. However, the record publishers refused their permission. An approach to the owner of the copyright in Arthur Sullivan's music would have been of no avail, because the record company owned that special right in the *actual recording*. Eventually, the problem was solved without the need for any pre-recordings: individuals who felt it absolutely necessary to listen to the recording outside of school hours simply borrowed a copy from their local public lending library.

Similar procedures apply to spoken word recordings. At one time, such items were generally popular as education tapes including recordings of lectures. These days, spoken word productions cover all manner of material from audio books, often read verbatim by a professional such as a member of Equity, through to papers given at seminars and conferences. So, again, if you wish to re-record, apply first of all to the recording company. If the publishing company passes your request over to the *speaker* for any copyright clearance in the material watch out for one possible snag: some spoken word tapes use music at the beginning and/or end of the production, which would almost certainly require additional copyright clearance.

To make things easier all round, most recording companies appoint an agency to act on their behalf, to issue permission, collect royalties and so on. Details are given on cassette and record labels. The most common are Mechanical-Copyright Protection Society, acting on behalf of music publishers, Phonographic Performance Limited (PPL), acting on behalf of record companies, and the Performing Right Society (PRS) which issues licences for the public performance of recorded works. The addresses of these and other pertinent organizations will be found in Appendix 2.

Rental right

Until only a few years ago we would probably not have considered rental rights in sound recordings. However, now there are organizations renting out compact discs, and soon we may also see digital audio tapes being rented out. In the light of developments, the 1988 Copyright, Designs and Patents Act allows the Secretary of State to introduce a sound recordings rental right at any time should such a step be considered necessary.

A rental right, if introduced, would come through the initiation of a Statutory Instrument approved by both Houses of Parliament. However, this would not be necessary if a licensing scheme were devised to licence the rental of sound recordings. Should either a rental right or an appropriate licensing scheme be introduced, its purpose would be to ensure that copyright owners receive a fair payment for their works which are rented out.

Amateur recording licence

In conjunction with the British Phonographic Industry, the Mechanical-Copyright Protection Society *used* to issue amateur recording licences. However, due to the very small number of people actually taking out the licence, MCPS was compelled to discontinue this service as far back as 1980.

Term of audio copyright

There has been considerable debate over the years relating to the period for which a sound recording may enjoy copyright protection. In 1961, an international convention was held in Rome to explore the far-reaching questions surrounding the copyright protection of performers, phonogram producers and broadcasters.

This discussion gave birth to what is commonly known as the *Rome Convention*; signatories to that Convention agreed that copyright protection for sound recordings (and, incidentally, broadcasts) should be for a minimum period of 20 years from the date the recording was made. It was also agreed that publishers of such recordings would do everything possible to ensure that the symbol ℗ together with the year of first publication would appear somewhere on the packaging of each recording.

The Rome Convention was not welcomed with open arms, as can be shown by the fact that only approximately 30 countries have added their names to its support.

However, the 1988 British legislation provides that the copyright term for audio recordings is a period of 50 years from the year of first publication.

Domestic copying machines

Although recent advances in technology are designed to make life easier for everyone, some advances have been hailed as detrimental to traders. Through the eyes of copyright owners, equipment such as contemporary twin-deck tape recorders are seen as incentives to members of the community to break the law by copying commercially produced audio cassettes. It has also been alleged that currently available equipment could also encourage the illegal copying of computer programs, video films, and so on.

Prior to the passing of the 1988 Act, the Government's White Paper suggested that a suitable course of action might well be to introduce a levy on blank audio cassettes. In return, the public would be able to make copies of commercially produced tapes and records, and proceeds from the levy would be distributed amongst copyright owners and performers.

However, at the end of the day, the blank tape levy scheme was dropped. This means that it remains illegal for any of us to make our own copies of commercially produced recordings, even for our own, individual private use!

With this in mind, some pressure groups are now more concerned than ever that the marketing of such machines as twin-deck tape recorders (particularly with a 'high-speed dubbing' facility), music centres, and the like, do nothing more than encourage people to infringe the copyright regulations, even though publicity and instruction manuals for such equipment generally carry a 'small print' reminder to the effect that it is illegal to copy the vast majority of recordings without a valid licence.

Two such pressure groups, the British Phonographic Industry and the Mechanical Rights Society, decided to make a test case of the issue. These two organizations jointly brought a case against the Amstrad Company, alleging that Amstrad were "inciting people to infringe copyright laws with the marketing of its twin cassette systems". The pressure groups, interestingly enough, lost their case, but took it to the Court of Appeal in March 1987. They lost their appeal, but did receive permission to take their case further, to the House of Lords. Following a rather lengthy legal process, the House of Lords ruled in 1988 in favour of Amstrad.

This case has served to demonstrate that it is perfectly reasonable for manufacturers and importers to supply equipment such as twin-cassette systems, and that members of the public are perfectly entitled to purchase and own such hardware. It is up to the user to make certain they are within the law if they do any copying!

It is probable that instances like this influenced the thinking of the

Department of Trade and Industry when they ensured that the 1988 Act allows for a copyright owner to apply for an order for the confiscation of any equipment that he or she has reason to believe was used to produce infringing copies of a work.

Public performance

No permission or licence is required if any audio recording is to be played within the confines of a club or society, or similar organization, so long as the institution concerned is *not* set up to be profit-making, *and* that its prime concerns are charitable and/or involved with propagating religion, education or social welfare. On any occasions when a charge is made for admission to an event where such a recording is to be played, it is a legal requirement that all the proceeds are provided as a direct contribution towards the objects of the organization in question. In effect, this means that sound recordings may be played in a church service of divine worship, or in a school or college as part of the teaching curriculum, or within a club or similar society with charitable objectives as part of the club's general programme.

In all other cases, a licence is required *before* a recording is played in public, and in most cases such a licence is available from the Performing Right Society.

Certain commercial organizations provide tapes for background atmosphere music in places such as restaurants and sports centres. Some of these concerns will arrange a PRS licence on your behalf, or may even hold a blanket licence, but do take the trouble to check with the representative of any such service that you may consider making use of. Never simply assume that you are covered! And if in doubt, remember it only takes one short telephone conversation with the Performing Right Society to check things out!

I am frequently asked about the situation as it applies to background music in public houses, hotels, etc. The position is that the Performing Right Society, in negotiation with the National Union of Licensed Victuallers (also representing the Scottish Licensed Trade Association), provides a licence tailor made to suit the requirements of these establishments. As far as is practicable, the royalties payable take into account the varying sizes of public houses.

Juke boxes in places such as public houses can also be covered by a PRS licence. It is possible to take out a PRS licence that is renewable annually, with a charge being levied for the main unit and a surcharge for each additional wall unit or coin-entry point.

For application forms and applicable charges, of any or all of the above-mentioned licence schemes, please contact the Performing Right Society whose address is provided in Appendix 2.

Radio broadcasts

Under the 1988 Copyright, Designs and Patents Act, the government has declared that copyright in a broadcast is not infringed by anyone making a recording of that broadcast for their own private purposes. It is believed that many citizens probably record radio broadcasts for one or both of two reasons. The first is to listen to a broadcast on a time-shift basis; perhaps the radio programme clashes with a television transmission, so they record the radio programme and listen to it at a later time, after which they re-use the tape for some other purpose.

The second prime use of off-air recording is by students who record their educational broadcasts so that they can listen to them again for revision. Again, the tape is re-used for some other purpose once their course of instruction has been completed.

Remember, when recording a radio broadcast, copyright is not infringed when the recording is only for the sole private use of the person making the recording. For any other use, permission from the radio station responsible for the original programme would be required.

Additionally, it is interesting to note that copyright is not infringed when a broadcast is heard in public by persons who have *not paid for admission* to the establishment where the broadcast may be heard. This implies, for example, that it would be permissible for a restaurant to have its radio on to provide background music provided that the customers were not being charged any extra for the privilege of listening to the broadcast.

Education

Educational establishments may record programmes for the purposes of their curriculum without infringing copyright *except* where broadcasts are covered by special licensing schemes. If in doubt about whether such a scheme exists to cover a particular programme, check with the radio station responsible for the original broadcast.

Audiovisual presentations

Audiovisual presentations are popular for sales conferences, training seminars, and so on. These presentations comprise the sequential screening of pictures (usually slide transparencies) married to a taped sound commentary.

The visual side of the presentation is often compiled from personal or specially commissioned photographs and illustrations; the audio counterpart could well be a personally dictated spoken-word commentary. In such instances, the chances are that the presenter owns most, if not all, of the copyrights involved.

In situations where either pictures or sound are to be obtained from another source, full copyright clearance must be obtained in advance of any presentation taking place. For this purpose, bear in mind that such presentations normally constitute public performance.

When putting together the soundtrack for any kind of audiovisual presentation, it is often useful to include some professionally recorded sound effects in order to enhance the production and stimulate interest from your audience. Pre-recorded records and tapes of a whole catalogue of sound effects from galloping horses to church bells, from thunder and lighting to gentle winds, are available on loan from many public lending libraries, or may be purchased from many high street shops. Most popular is probably the complete series of sound effects records produced by the British Broadcasting Corporation and released by BBC Enterprises, although similar recordings have also been released by such organizations as Thorn-EMI. The copyright in these recordings is, of course, vested in the record publishing companies, but most such recordings are available for amateur use without the necessity to obtain special permission. However, it is absolutely imperative to obtain a licence for the use of such material for any professional or commercial purpose.

Other sound reproductions

Recent electronic developments include domestic items which, however vaguely, utilize some form of sound recording and reproduction.

Amongst the more popular are the modern equivalents of door bells for houses and flats. Many versions include one or more musical melodies on either a microchip memory or an endless loop cassette.

Then there are the increasingly ubiquitous musical boxes. Originally produced as clockwork mechanical devices, today's counterparts tend to come as battery powered electronic items. Whether offered as children's toys or grown-up's trinket boxes, they all incorporate a reproduction of a well-known melody.

Less popular, perhaps, than the items described above, but none-the-less just as important from the point of view of copyright, are general toys and souvenirs that recreate in an audible fashion the melody of a well-known tune. In fact, many such novelties operate in a similar fashion to musical boxes, and could probably be classified as such.

More up-market goods, often described as 'executive toys', include machines designed to provide music-on-hold for telephone callers. Such machines must not be overlooked because although their use is mainly with business at present, domestic versions are available and some suppliers expect the domestic use (as well as the business use) of such machines will escalate within the next few years. Basically music-on-hold machines provide music along telephone lines to callers who are obliged to hold on until the person or department that they are calling is available, thus assuring them that they haven't been cut off and also (possibly) entertaining them.

Industrial machines operate by playing the music automatically as soon as the operator has put the caller on hold on either private automatic branch exchange (PABX) systems or on the less sophisticated key systems. Some of the more expensive domestic telephone models also incorporate a unique music-on-hold feature. The business machines often operate from an endless-loop tape cassette, which enables the cassettes and tunes to be changed from time to time.

All these uses of music, and any others that may have occurred to you, have just one thing on common: copyright. Many manufacturers take great care to utilize non-copyright tunes whenever possible, but there are always the exceptions when copyright music is used.

The vast majority of musical copyright owners in the United Kingdom are full members of the Mechanical-Copyright Protection Society. This society is able to provide licences for irregular miscellaneous uses of its members' works. As each such use varies, often considerably, from the next, it is necessary to write to MCPS Licensing Department, explaining exactly what use you have in mind for whichever pieces of music you deem appropriate, and indicate the approximate time in minutes and seconds that you anticipate each extract of music might take. MCPS will then consider your request and, if acceptable, advise you of the appropriate charges.

Piracy of tapes and records

Thanks to the huge investments of audio tape publishers, record companies and distributors, the range of pre-recorded titles available for our enjoyment is constantly on the increase.

The vast majority of pre-recorded audio products are of music, or include music as part of the programme offered. Initially, the composers will have spent many costly hours in perfecting their work to an acceptably high standard. Once a contract has been signed, publishers will part with thousands of pounds to cover studio time and mastering alone. Further investment is called for to cover packaging and sleeve designs, advertising and promotional charges, and distributions to the retail stores of the finished audio cassettes, records and compact discs. When we consider that some audio products of popular music are promoted by videos, it is no surprise to learn that the promotional costs can be remarkably high.

These large budgets have encouraged some producers to come together to form the United Kingdom Anti-Piracy Group. They have also let it be known that they consider international piracy to be a particular threat to their livelihood.

Nobody wins when an infringing (or illegal) copy of any audio product is made and sold. In the mid 1980s it was estimated that British publishers lost millions of pounds of potential income due to the bootleggers, and that estimate was made as a result of looking at just a handful of the world's publishing territories. The loss to the British economy in terms of foreign earnings, tax payments, etc. may be measured by noting that British music recordings alone account for over 20 per cent of all record sales worldwide!

Like book publishers, publishers of audio cassettes, tapes and discs have been known to take action against those suspected of flaunting copyright legislation. Legal proceedings have resulted in the confiscation of bootleg items. Stiffer penalties are expected as a consequence of the Copyright, Designs and Patents Act 1988.

5
Television and video _____

It has not taken many years for video to develop from a high-technology concept to become a household toy. Mechanically operated video tape recorders have joined the ranks of the extinct, giving way to sophisticated electronic, microcomputer assisted, video cassette machines. Home video systems have been among the fastest selling pieces of electronic gadgetry in the late 1980s, and the time is fast approaching when virtually every home will have one.

We have already seen how new technology brings not only new opportunities but also new problems. The rapid spread of relatively cheap video equipment is inevitably accompanied by a web of copyright legality red tape waiting to ensnare the unsuspecting member of the public!

And what a web it is. Let us look at those points that are most likely to arise and affect us under current legislation.

Television programmes

A major reason for the popularity of domestic video cassette recorders is that people wish to record their favourite television programmes. They record programmes that are being transmitted when they are out, so that they can watch their idols at a later time, then re-use the tape for a similar exercise another day. The video recorder also resolves the problem of the inevitable clash in timing between two favourite programmes on different channels. This is a problem that may grow as the number of available channels increases.

It is gratifying to note that the Department of Trade and Industry realised the importance of this use, and in the 1988 Act declared that copyright is not infringed by private persons making video recordings of television and cable broadcasts, taking such recordings off-air for their own private purposes at home. By implication, this must include transmissions received via satellite broadcasting, since such broadcasting is of television programmes.

In effect, the government has cleared the air for the benefit of those who do undertake time-shift recording of TV programmes. It has, however, been made quite clear that recordings of television transmissions may not be further copied, sold, screened in public, re-broadcast, and so on, without the prior licence of the copyright owners and programme makers. All copyright in broadcast material remains the property of the author and/or composer, or any other party to whom the work may have been assigned. Furthermore, there is also a separate copyright in the actual original recording or broadcast which is owned by the production company.

The 1988 UK legislation provides that copyright in a work is not infringed by its *incidental* inclusion in an artistic work, sound recording, film, broadcast or cable programme. This suggests, for example, that copyright in a painting or photograph would not be infringed in a television broadcast, if it could be demonstrated that the picture was incidentally displayed in a room from whence the transmission was originating. On the other hand, if it could be shown that a copyright work was deliberately included in the transmission, without prior permission, then a definite violation of copyright would have occurred.

From all this, it would appear advisable that should you have some reason for using a videotape you have made of a television broadcast, other than privately at home, you should write first to the producer of the programme to check exactly what permissions you require. Copyrights in television programmes can be extremely complex, bearing in mind that in just one short transmission there could be a cocktail of background music, poetry, quotation from a book, perhaps some drama, a painting, a photograph and so on. There might even be a case for you having to pay a royalty to persons appearing in the programme.

It is unlawful to make an unauthorized copy of a cinematograph film, but since UK legislation permits the private recording of television transmissions, *presumably* this must include films that are shown on the small screen. And if it does then, again, use is restricted to private viewing by yourself in your own home. Indeed, the presumption about domestic time-shift recording of films is sometimes cited as a selling point by salespersons. One of the purveyors of satellite television receiving systems, Satellite Technology Systems, actually suggest in a promotional leaflet that you use your video recorder in conjunction with your satellite receiving system "to record a good movie from one of the film channels during the day so you could enjoy watching it that evening". The leaflet doesn't actually mention copyright but, of course, if you should be in any doubt whatever the proper course of action would be to write to the distributor of the film in question to seek clarification. The film distributor's address can usually be obtained from the television company responsible for giving it airtime.

Registered Open University students have always been permitted to record OU television programmes that are relevant to their particular courses, on condition that they use such tapes only for the purpose of their own private study. Other viewers have been able to obtain recording licences from Open University Education Enterprises at Milton Keynes. However, now that we have the 1988 Act clearly stating that no prior licence is required for the purposes of domestic off-air recording of television broadcasts, it is necessary to obtain permission only for recording that is other than time-shift recording for your personal viewing.

Television programmes received either via satellite or through cable distribution attract similar rights to those of more conventional transmission.

Teletext transmissions are treated, for the purposes of copyright, in exactly the same way as other television services. One of the fruits of recent technology is the development of equipment that enables teletext sub-titles to be recorded on video tape for the benefit of deaf viewers.

Educational television

Major television programme makers produce material suitable for students' studies. Many television stations designate a good deal of their output specifically for use in schools and other educational establishments. Some of these establishments have found it desirable to record some transmissions off-air, especially for showing to students whose timetables exclude their availability at the exact time of the original transmission.

Obviously, these seats of learning do not come under the classification of being private persons recording for their own private purposes. However, the government has shown that it is sympathetic towards educational establishments by recognizing that many television programmes and cable broadcasts contain much of academic value. Accordingly, the 1988 Act provides that copyright is not infringed by an educational establishment (school, college, university, etc.) recording a television programme or cable broadcast specifically for use within its educational curriculum.

This privilege, however, applies only to those transmissions that do not happen to be covered by any licensing schemes. This is an extremely important point to bear in mind, because over the past decade or so, notably prior to the passage through Parliament of the present legislation, television companies demonstrated their concern for the educational fraternity, one result being that the major companies introduced their own licensing schemes in order to assist schools and colleges.

The *British Broadcasting Corporation* permit educational institutions to record off-air those programmes which, in their weekly journal the *Radio Times*, have been marked with *(e)* for 'educational'. These are basically BBC educational programmes other than Open University programmes, and full details are provided in the BBC's *Annual Programmes* leaflet which is sent to all schools and other educational bodies. This arrangement is subject to a number of conditions, including that only one copy is made of any transmission, that the copy will be used for instructional purposes in class, and that each recording is destroyed after a specified period. Complete details are available to teachers and lecturers in a leaflet *Recording BBC Educational Programmes*, which may be obtained on request from the BBC Copyright Department (see Appendix 2 for the address).

It must be emphasized that the arrangements made by the BBC do not also apply to the educational output of the various independent television companies. There are, in fact, no less than three separate schemes covering the various educational programmes broadcast by independent television.

First, there is the *Independent Television Association* (formerly the Independent Television Companies Association) annual licence. This licence is available to local education authorities. Off-air recordings of educational programmes only may be made in any educational institution in the area of a local education authority which holds a current valid ITV Association Education Programme Recording Licence. As well as being restricted to educational transmissions, the ITV Association licence covers only programmes broadcast on the local independent television station, certain Channel Four transmissions, but not any other channels. Each recording made off-air may be retained for a period of three years, and may be used in *any* educational institution within the geographical area and control of the licensed local education authority.

The Independent Television Association is happy to receive applications for analogous licences from independent educational bodies, or from educational institutions whose local education authority may not hold a current ITV Association licence. The nominal charge for this licence, at the time of going to press, is £5. Full details regarding the licence, and licence application forms, are available from the Education Officer at the Independent Television Association, whose address will be found in Appendix 2.

Secondly, there is the *London Weekend Television* Licensing Scheme. LWT's licence is also issued annually, and is available to both educational and training institutions. This licence provides for off-air recorded use of all transmissions of a particular series, produced by London Weekend Television, in which educational and training bodies have expressed an interest. At the time of going to press, licences were available for the following three series: *Weekend World* (LWT), *Credo* (C4) and *The London Programme* (LWT London area).

For up to date details of which series are currently covered by the LWT licence, transmission dates and times, and licence fees, please contact London Weekend Television at the address in Appendix 2.

Finally, there's the situation relating to *Channel Four*. Educational programmes are produced for Channel Four by the various independent television companies and, as a consequence, the ITV Association licence described above covers the off-air recording of many educational programmes transmitted by Channel Four. All programmes covered by the ITV Association licence are indicated by an *E* symbol in the Independent Broadcasting Authority's booklet *TV Take-up*, which is published annually. Copies of the booklet are available upon request from the IBA.

To cover all other Channel Four educational programmes, a Channel Four Television Recording Licence scheme has been set up. The scheme is administered, on behalf of Channel Four, by Guild Learning. Programmes covered by this licence are indicated in *TV Take-up* by a *G* symbol, are publicized from time to time in the *Times Educational Supplement*, and are also announced on the 4-Tel teletext service.

Issued annually, the Channel Four licence registration fee varies in accordance with both the category of user (e.g. schools, churches, community groups, colleges, teachers' centres, industrial training bodies) and also the type of programmes the user intends to record. Tapes of programmes recorded may be retained for one year, but it is possible for users to pay a fee in order to gain entitlement to retain specific tapes for a further period of twelve months.

Full details of the Channel Four licence scheme, including current fees covering various categories of users, are obtainable from the Channel Four TV Recording Licence Department at the address given in Appendix 2.

Educational videos

Video publishing is now with us to stay, but it is no longer restricted to the entertainment and leisure markets. Many publishers, several of whom are members of the *Educational Publishers Council*, have produced video cassettes that are oriented to educational needs, and some of these are available for purchase at high street shops as well as through suppliers of educational books and materials.

Many educational videos have been prepared to back up the more conventional learning packages consisting of textbooks and work-books. Such videos have been found to encourage children's learning, not least because many of them spend a lot of time in front of the small screen at home. It has been suggested that interactive video programmes will be listed among the most popular of teaching resources in the early 21st century; on the other hand, electronics technology is progressing at such a pace that some more advanced resources might well be in vogue by then!

Scholarly lessons on video cassettes are intended to be viewed within the classroom situation. They may also be viewed privately by a purchaser at his home address, but any other form of presentation requires permission to be obtained in advance. Some teachers have been known to ask of producers if they can make a 'back-up' copy, lest the original be wiped accidentally. Replies to such requests are generally negative. The cassettes have their recording tabs removed, rendering inadvertent over-recording an impossibility.

Publishers involved in releasing educational videos generally include full information about their activities in their mailings to schools.

More than 4500 films and videos are available for screening in primary and/or secondary schools. The British Film Institute (address in Appendix 2) has endeavoured to put together as much information about these titles as it can, which has resulted in *Films and Videograms for Schools*, a two-volume publication available by mail order from the BFI. As can be expected, the volumes cover a wide mix of material from hundreds of sources. In addition to educational programmes, sponsored and independent productions, a number of feature films are included in the listings. Around one-fifth of the titles listed are indicated as being available on free loan.

Recording with a video camera

Many amateur photographers are now discarding their Instamatics, and retiring their home movie gear, in favour of a home video camera. This boasts the advantages that the video recordings are instantly playable, and if they are not also commendable the tape may be re-used. In fact, home video taping is so convenient that one can be far more adventurous than might ever have been considered with, say, 8 mm home movie outfits.

For the average home video enthusiast, getting the family holiday down on tape, or recording animal antics on that outing to the zoo, or recording a mock television interview with Cousin Sid, are all perfectly acceptable, and should not require any copyright permissions. Of course, the tape that you have shot is your copyright, and anyone wishing to make a copy of it, or use it in any way, must seek out your permission. For example, if you happen to be recording your family enjoying themselves on holiday when the hotel over the road suddenly bursts into flames, the chances are that you will turn your camera onto the unfortunate event. When a *News At Ten* reporter arrives on the scene to find that you've captured the prime news of the day on video tape, he will almost certainly wish to negotiate to use your tape on the news. Such items are usually flashed with the words 'amateur video' when transmitted.

The most common uses of amateur video recording are weddings and other church services, school plays performed for the benefit of the parents and productions of the local amateur dramatic and music societies.

For weddings and other church events, permission for video taping (as for filming) in or around church premises needs to be obtained in advance from the minister in charge. Strictly speaking, you also require the permission of *every* participant in the service. However, it is generally acknowledged that this is rather cumbersome and taking matters to extreme! Don't assume, incidentally, that the priest or minister in charge will automatically grant permission for video taping in their church. In February 1983, the *Daily Mail* reported that a group of clergymen in the Warrington area had jointly taken a decision to ban all video taping of weddings at their various churches. It seems that the churches in question were worried lest any copyright, or other, law should be violated, however unintentionally. Other churches have been known to refuse video taping permission, reserving their right not to indicate the reason.

Queries have been raised from time to time as to why some churches have been known to refuse permission for video taping wedding and other services, but at the same time raised no objection to photographs being taken of the event. A possible answer lies in the fact that video tapes include a soundtrack, and contrary to popular belief much of the music used in churches is fully protected by copyright. Remember, for example, that even older pieces of liturgical music may well have recent arrangements that are still in copyright. The Mechanical-Copyright Protection Society is the principal agent for copyright music, and you may apply direct to it (address in Appendix 2) for a licence. The MCPS licence covers only music for which the copyright is owned by members of that society, but as virtually all music copyright owners are members, it is unlikely that churches (or other organizations) will be using music not covered by MCPS. The MCPS licence fee to cover music used at weddings and similar events is, at the time of going to press, £5 plus VAT. The licence covers the recording of one original tape plus nine copies, on condition that no copies are sold or used for any commercial purposes.

Some photographers and video companies are now offering a commercial service to make video tapes of weddings. To cover this new industry, MCPS has introduced an annual 'company' licence. Holders of such a licence do not have to go to the expense and trouble of having to obtain a separate licence for every wedding they record on video tape. This is helpful for the entrepreneur who may be undertaking several commissions each month. To obtain such a licence, it is necessary to complete a form and pay the fee! The commercial licensing scheme form is available upon request from the video department at MCPS, and details of current fees are supplied with each form.

A few years ago, I heard about a couple who had their wedding ceremony video taped. The church organist subsequently claimed that as his talent was to be heard on the soundtrack of the tape, he should receive some payment under the Performers' Protection Act. The couple refused to make any payment to him, but wondered exactly what the legal position was.

At the time, this query embodied a grey area of legislation in the Performers' Protection Acts 1958–72. However, these Acts are all repealed by the Copyright, Designs and Patents Act 1988, which provides us with a far clearer statement: a person may make a recording of the performer, without the performer's consent, if the recording is for the maker's private and domestic use. So, assuming that the recording of the wedding was purely for the happy couple to remind themselves of their vows at some later date, there would be no problems under present legislation.

Another couple who had their marriage vows recorded onto videotape wanted to dub onto the video soundtrack some music from a record. In order to do this and remain on the right side of the law, they wrote to the publisher of the record, explaining the circumstances, and requesting the appropriate permission. The music in question was out of copyright, otherwise they would also have required authority from the copyright owner.

Local amateur drama groups and operatic societies like to have their performances video taped for the purpose of self-criticism and evaluation and as a training tool to help them polish up their performances, so upgrading their presentation and image. Once the cast have had the opportunity to see themselves, the tape is stored away for re-use at the next event. So long as the video tapes are kept within the confines of such self-training exercises, and viewed only in private by the cast, then this is considered to be a matter 'of education and training, and no copyright permissions would be deemed necessary.

On the other hand, an amateur group that commissions the making of a video tape recording of one of their presentations in order to have copies made for however limited a distribution, and possibly to boost their local funds or even in aid of a charitable cause, would need to obtain prior permission from the copyright owners of the work in question. As a general rule publishers of the majority of plays, musicals, etc., either own the copyright or act as agents for the copyright owners. In the first instance, you should therefore write to the publisher, explaining exactly what you have in mind and that it is a completely amateur production. Usually, permission is granted in return for the payment of a royalty for each copy of the video tape that you have made.

An increasing number of schools boast an amateur video camera amongst their inventory. Such schools like to record the annual school play for much the same reasons as amateur dramatic societies. Some fortunate pupils gain the opportunity to learn how to use the camera, and employ their new-found talent to assist their classmates in the drama group. Copies of these school videos are rarely made for sale purposes, public viewing or broadcasting, although the situation could change as equipment (and children) becomes more sophisticated. In such cases, the rules applicable to local drama groups, outlined above, should be followed.

It was once suggested to me that because a musical happened to be staged in a church hall, no permission would be needed to video tape the presentation as it was taking place on church premises, but there is no let-out here. Permission from the copyright owner is always required irrespective of the type of premises used.

Some churches make video recordings of their Sunday services for playing back to people unable to be present, e.g. housebound senior citizens or members in hospital. If your church is either involved with, or is considering the possibility of starting, such a 'video ministry', remember that you do require prior permission to video tape any work, or extract of any work, that may be used during a service. The best plan is to ensure that the church council, or equivalent committee, plan their orders of service several weeks ahead. This should guarantee that you have a reasonable time to ensure that you have any appropriate permissions in the bag; such a plan further provides time to change a proposed item in the unfortunate event of a request for permission to use it being turned down.

Private functions

A very real problem that has arisen recently is that of 'actuality' music that is recorded onto the soundtrack of an amateur video recording of a private function. By this, we mean music that is in any way audible at the event, or in the building, where the video filming is taking place. The 1988 Act provides that incidental recording of such copyright material is *not* an infringement of copyright law.

To cover places such as discotheques, where the music is obviously a proper part of the recording, MCPS offers an *actuality music* licence, applicable to amateur videos only. It is necessary to complete an application form to obtain an actuality music licence, and such forms are available upon request from MCPS, telephone number 01–769 4400 (address in Appendix 2). Note that the MCPS licence covers only copyright musical works. For copyright sound recordings (such as played at a disco) an additional licence is available from Phonographic Performance (01–437 0311).

After you have shot your video, you may desire to dub some music onto the soundtrack, perhaps as background or mood music. A list of organizations operating sound music libraries is in Appendix 3. MCPS is able to provide licences for the use of such music for video recordings of private functions and for audiovisual presentations.

Public performance

Inevitably, in any consideration of copyright, there is a sharp distinction between private use and public use. Suppose you were to hire a video cassette of a feature film from your local video library. You then booked a public hall and put the word around that you were going to show the film at that hall. If you did so, you would actually be putting on a public performance of that film, and unless you had made prior arrangements with the copyright owners, i.e. the producers and/or distributors of that film, you would be breaking the law.

Video tapes stocked by video libraries for loan to the public are rented out on condition that they are only used privately in the homes of persons hiring them. The same applies to pre-recorded video cassettes offered for sale in retail shops; they are sold to be played back only in the privacy of the buyer's own home.

It is possible, however, to arrange public screenings of videos, by writing direct to the distributor, explaining the circumstances and why you wish to show a particular item publicly (e.g. in aid of new, vital equipment for the local hospital). If there are no copyright restrictions or other objections to what you have in mind, a *public performance* copy will be loaned to you. Some commercial organizations, such as Shell UK and British Gas, have produced films and video recordings that may be borrowed for public performances. Details of such organizations are to be found in most public reference libraries, and they will be pleased to supply their catalogues of available programmes.

Some video distributors who possess film rights in addition to their video rights, might suggest that you use the cinematograph film version rather than a video, the argument being that a film is the most suitable for large screen presentation. In this case, you should weigh up all the pros and cons, taking into full account the size of your auditorium, the anticipated number of people expected to make up your audience, the equipment available to you, and, of course, your budget.

Remember that, as long as you have accounted for it in your budget, it is now possible to hire video projectors and large video screens, and increasingly, this concoction of hardware is being produced to high definition standards (although, for large audiences, the quality of film has not yet been surpassed). Many hotels and conference centres are equipped with video tape screening equipment which is available to organizations hiring rooms for their events, large and small. And a video recorder is less complicated to operate than a film projector.

As always, there are apparent 'grey' areas. Does, for example, showing a video in a school count as a public performance; after all, there might be as many as 30 pupils in a class, as opposed to only three or four people in one's own family at home? The fact is that a school is an educational establishment and would be entitled to show a video to its scholars, as part of the teaching curriculum – for the purposes of education, incidentally, not for entertainment!

But suppose a school's Parent Teacher Association decide to screen a video programme, probably outside normal school hours, as a fund-raising exercise. Even though the programme is being shown in the school building, this would constitute a public performance, and the PTA would need to obtain the appropriate licence before setting the event up.

Then there are difficulties surrounding religious organizations, especially churches and Sunday schools. Could somebody be breaking the law by showing a video production in a church, or by showing a television programme in Sunday school that's been recorded off-air?

Let's deal with Sunday schools first. This category of users certainly does constitute a 'grey' area. On one hand, it would appear illegal to record a television transmission off-air for screening to children in a Sunday school, without prior permission from the television company concerned, because only personal recording for private purposes in one's own home is allowed. On the other hand, it is obvious to many that Sunday schools are educational establishments, since their purpose is to provide Christian (or religious) education. Indeed, state primary education evolved from the early Sunday school movement pioneered by Robert Raikes in the late eighteenth century.

The question that presents itself so forcibly, therefore, is whether or not a twentieth century Sunday school could claim to be an 'educational establishment' for the purposes of the latest UK copyright legislation? If it could, then it could claim similar rights to day schools and colleges (see earlier in this chapter, under *Educational television*). My personal view, however, in the absence of a test case, is that Sunday schools should *not* claim the rights appropriate to educational establishments. Times have changed since 200 years ago, and Sunday schools no longer teach reading and writing!

It is relevant to note that current UK legislation maintains that copyright is not infringed when a television or cablevision transmission is viewed by an audience who have not paid for admission to the premises on which the programme is seen. This *implies* that if a programme suitable for Sunday schools is being transmitted during Sunday school hours, it would be possible for the Sunday school attenders to view it on a convenient television set without needing prior authority.

Churches, and other places of worship, are yet another kettle of fish! Because they are, by their nature, freely open to members of the public, any showing of any video production whatever must clearly be seen as constituting a public performance.

Realizing the potential of the church market alongside the even greater potential for Christian ministry and mission through the medium of video, all the major religious film producers have now transferred the majority of their films onto video cassettes. Many new productions are automatically produced in video format. A large number of new, smaller producers are emerging with their own religious videos. Many of these organizations hire or sell their productions with the intention that they be screened on church premises; churches therefore do not have to obtain any special licences or other authorization to show such videos publicly.

It must be realised, however, that the number of video productions intended for screening on church premises is strictly limited! Many religious videos carry similar small print to the secular ones, indicating that such videos are restricted to private home viewing only and that any other manner of exhibition, including public performance, without prior written consent of the copyright holder or agent, constitutes an infringement of copyright.

Incidentally, some of those organizations that provide videos for church use also supply publicity handouts that can easily be overprinted with details of the local 'premiere' or event. Details of several thousand Christian video productions and their suppliers are to be found in the *Guide to Christian Video* (Jay books).

Making a television programme

With the advent of cable and satellite transmissions on an entreprenurial scale to domestic users within the United Kingdom and the planned relaxation of control on the conventional broadcast channels, a second generation of lively television programme makers is mushrooming. Domestic receiving dishes springing up around Britain are seen by many as the opening door to a potentially vast new industry: small programme makers with big expectations. These new producers aim to make a selection of programmes that they can sell to transmitting companies, or with a view to buying time to get their material broadcast.

At the moment in Britain, budding programme makers have no option other than to use their selling charms on the various transmitting or distributing companies. Most are hoping that the time will come when they can actually buy time on British television just as they can in, say, the United States of America. Meanwhile, the outlook is a little brighter for those smaller, community producers who are involved with making programmes of local interest. With the advent of local television channels transmitted on a microwave network (Multipoint Video Distribution System), coupled with local cable transmissions, their programmes are fast gaining the opportunity to be aired.

Many of these programmes are magazine style, the video track of the recordings being the original property of the production company. But included in the amalgam of different elements of copyright that make up a television programme there is, more often than not, a certain amount of canned background music selected to help the viewer enter into the mood of the transmission.

This dubbed soundtrack demands just as much care in checking copyright clearance as the video track. It is easy to assume that a recording of a non-copyright work requires no permission for its use when, in fact, the recording could be of a copyright arrangement. Of course, any copyright holder maintains the liberty to refuse permission, but my experience is that permission is generally given.

Major British national organizations such as the British Broadcasting Corporation and the Independent Television Association have blanket agreements with the Mechanical-Copyright Protection Society covering copyright music, but it should be noted that these arrangements cover only programmes originated by those organizations. So if, for example, you are making a programme that you hope to sell to Channel Four, you will still need to obtain your own copyright clearances in respect of any music used in addition to any other copyright permissions that may be involved.

The Mechanical-Copyright Protection Society has more than 10 000 members who are owners of musical copyrights, and it has offered, on behalf of those members, to advise UK production companies on matters pertaining to music that they may wish to include in the soundtracks of their original programmes. In the first instance, telephone their Licensing Department on 01–769 4400.

Promotional video

Video promotions in high street stores provide manufacturers and distributors with a popular method of advertising their wares. The products demonstrated in such presentations are, generally, the copyright of the promoter, thus covering the rights involved in the video track. But, again, music is often used on the soundtrack.

To make life easier for the producers of such videos, the MCPS Video Department provides a service for the copyright clearance of sound recordings to manufacturers of in-store videograms.

A recent innovation is for manufacturers to offer to members of the public special video tapes in full or part redemption of proofs of purchase. MCPS offers a tailor-made *Premium Videogram Licence* to cover its members' music used on the soundtrack. Producers of such videos should contact MCPS direct in order to obtain details pertinent to their specific requirements.

Rental right

The explosion in the numbers of video lending libraries in the mid-1980s, when it seemed that every petrol filling station and newsagent had become an agency, gave concern to copyright owners who realized that while the public were paying to hire their works, they (the copyright owners) were not receiving any financial reward, other than the royalty due at the time the libraries purchased copies of their works.

Understandably, therefore, provision has been incorporated into the 1988 Copyright, Designs and Patents Act for the Secretary of State to introduce formally some form of rental right, should he decide that this is necessary.

Video piracy

Only a few years ago, in early 1983, producers of videograms (the commercial term for pre-recorded video tapes, cassettes and discs) estimated that something like one million pounds was being spent

The Video Pirate

weekly by the public in the United Kingdom who were unwittingly purchasing *pirate videos*. In other words, because we had no way of knowing, we were buying illegal video tape copies of films and television programmes that had found their way into the commercial market place.

Currently, authentic videos often have some sort of security marking on them. This could be a special label, including a security hologram, or even a unique security stamp that can only be read with the aid of an ultraviolet lamp.

Video piracy is always investigated when members of the public suspect that they might have been sold an illegal video and report the matter, in confidence, to the Trading Standards Department of their local authority. (Pirate copies of videos are generally of inferior quality, and usually sold at prices well below the recommended retail prices of authentic equivalents.) An alternative is to report the matter by telephone to the Video Trade Association on 01–464 8833. Such reports are always investigated in complete confidence. Whenever video pirates are traced, prosecution is the inevitable result. Penalties imposed by the courts on the guilty are now heavier then ever before.

Real top-heavy investment comes into its own when we see just how much it costs to produce films and videos. We reach six-figure sums even for what are described as 'low budget' productions! With budgets like this at risk, British producers of films and videograms have got together with other British publishers of copyright works and formed UKAPG, the *United Kingdom Anti-Piracy Group*.

6
Microcomputers

Computers for general use were still at an early stage of development in the early 1950s. Consequently, the Copyright Act of 1956 made no specific mention of computer programming. Nevertheless, reading between the lines, it was quite clear that such programs do attract copyright protection, and to make it clear beyond doubt, the government introduced the Copyright (Computer Software) Amendment Act in 1985. This Amendment Act emphasized that all computer programs attract copyright protection, and that the person responsible for creating a program is the original copyright owner in similar fashion to a composer who owns the copyright in their musical composition.

Prior to the 1985 Amendment Act, copyright could legally subsist only after an idea had been produced in a tangible format, e.g. written down on paper. As soon as the 1985 Amendment Act became law, this changed so that copyright was able to subsist from the time when an idea had been committed either to a tangible format *or* encoded in some other (retrievable) way. In practice, this implied that any work created directly into a computer memory (i.e. by typing a program in from the computer keyboard, even though that program has not been written down on paper) immediately gains copyright protection.

This legislation also served to make it abundantly clear that the storing of a work in a computer memory (from which it would be possible to produce a hard copy or display a page on a visual display unit) is legally a form of reproduction that would require the copyright owner's prior consent.

Although both the 1956 Copyright Act and the 1985 Copyright (Computer Software) Amendment Act have now passed into history, having been repealed by the 1988 Copyright, Designs and Patents Act, both were hailed as important stepping stones towards the new legislation which states that, for the purposes of copyright law, a computer program must be considered as and treated as a 'literary work'. As with other works, copyright does not subsist in a computer program until it has been recorded 'in writing or otherwise'.

Many computer programs nowadays are actually compiled by assembling units taken from other previously written programs. If you compile a new program in this way, using previous programs of your own original making, of which you therefore own the copyright, this is perfectly in order. But it would appear that any segments of programs used that are copyright to other parties would necessitate you obtaining written permission from each and every one of those other parties. Your new program, albeit a compilation, would be your copyright, but if you wished to make copies of it, for any purpose, you would again need permission (and maybe even be required to pay royalties) to those who own the various copyrights that you have 'borrowed'.

So, apart from ensuring that there can be no misunderstanding over the fact that all computer programs are fully protected by copyright, the very latest legislation incorporates the far-reaching doctrine that copyright subsists in works fixed in any form from which they can in principle be reproduced. This must come as welcome news indeed for those copyright holders who have invested many years, and no doubt considerable sums of money, in their particular intellectual creations.

Programs

Microcomputer programs are generally available on either magnetic disk or compact cassette. By having two machines, e.g. two cassette tape recorders, linked up it is a simple matter to make copies of such programs. However, as has been seen above, such duplicating of computer programs without obtaining prior consent is illegal. If you require to make copies of any commercially produced programs, you must seek permission in advance by writing to the publisher of the program(s) in question. Of course, you do not need to write for specific permission to produce a back-up copy if a statement accom-

panies your program which clearly grants authority to make such a copy.

For non-commercially produced programs, e.g. a program written by a friend or member of a local computer group, you must obtain permission from the author of the program you wish to copy.

It has been suggested that it might not be necessary to obtain prior consent to make one copy of programs issued on either compact cassette or disk. The argument appears to be that it's sensible to have a 'back-up' copy of a computer program in case of loss of, or damage to, the original. Teachers and lecturers have put forward a good case for back-up copies, and this educational use is discussed in the next section. However, it seems to me that there is no doubt that any domestic or other private copying of programs, for whatever reason, is an infringement of copyright unless permission to copy has been obtained in writing beforehand.

Unfortunately, there are no definite guidelines laid down to assist suppliers of software to users who have several computers at their disposal. This aspect applies mainly (if not solely) to business users, as it is unlikely that other users will have the facilities afforded through owning or leasing a bank of computers. As a consequence, some suppliers of business software state in their terms of supply that each program is limited in use to just one computer. Thus a company boasting a whole network of computers would find itself having to make additional payments to cover a licence for each additional machine they wished to use each program on. In this situation, the suppliers of the software often ask their customers to specify the actual machine on which they intend to use specific programs.

What is being highlighted in such instances is the fact that, once a piece of software has been conveyed to a computer memory, that program is capable of being reproduced, even if only in some sort of electronic jargon. Such use therefore contravenes copyright legislation if it is undertaken without prior permission. In effect, any unauthorized downloading of any software, of any kind, must be seen to be illegal.

When suppliers of software specify the actual computer on which the purchaser may run a particular program, they are offering the user a *machine licence*. Holders of a machine licence have bought a computer program but their use of that program is restricted to a named computer.

On the other end of the scale comes what is commonly described as a *site licence*. This is a licence acquired by those buyers of a program who negotiate its use on all the computers they own, and which are installed at just one named address, or site. To use the same program on computers at some other address would necessitate either obtaining permission from the software publisher to make a copy or, more practicably, purchasing a second copy of the program, possibly with a site licence for use on all computers owned and installed at the second address.

Educational programs

Since the widespread introduction of microcomputers in schools, teachers have wished to be able to make at least one copy of every computer program they purchase for use in their teaching curriculum. They argue that such 'back-up' copies would only be used in case of emergency, e.g. should the original get damaged or corrupted during a class lecture, so that teaching may continue with the least possible disruption.

Publishers of educational programs have listened sympathetically to such requests. One of the major educational publishers of micro programs for use in schools and colleges is Longman Education. Their solution is to make duplicate copies available of each of their programs. Some publishers offer to sell to schools 'second' copies of their programs at a low price: this is an excellent idea, because it also means that teachers do not have to waste their valuable time producing their own back-up copies.

If you're a teacher and you wish to make a copy of any programs used at your school, do not hesitate to approach the publisher for permission if the literature accompanying the original fails to make it clear whether or not you are allowed to do so.

At the moment, there is no blanket licensing scheme available that covers the copying of microcomputer programs, although such a scheme could be introduced in the future, possibly run by an existing body such as the Copyright Licensing Agency.

Firmware

Contrary to rumours, *firmware* is not some cocktail of software and hardware that happens to be the property of a commercial firm. Firmware is, in fact, the common name ascribed to a permanent (therefore *firm*) item of what otherwise would be software. The most common forms of firmware are permanent programs built into a computer chip or into a *read only memory*, or ROM.

In the book trade, for example, booksellers and others may subscribe to Whitaker's *Books in Print* on CD-ROM. Subscribers to this service receive a regular mailing of the journal published on a compact disc (CD) and can bring up the information inscribed on the disc by means of a special player. Incidentally, *Books in Print* is also available as an annual service of four large printed books, and on monthly updated microfiche. The publishers discovered that subscribers to the microfiche version often pass on back issues at a cheap rate, but they do not anticipate the establishment of such a second-hand business with the CD-ROM version as this has a special protection device incorporated at the time of manufacture, known as *Time Out*. Basically, the Time Out protection is claimed to render superseded compact discs impossible to use.

As firmware consists of computer programs, copyright in all firmware subsists, as with other software, for a period of 50 years from the end of the calendar year in which a particular program was created.

Apart from that 50 year period, firmware enjoys similar copyright protection to, say, books or recordings: each item attracts copyright protection under the current legislation, and no reproduction or storage in any form whatsoever is allowed unless prior written permission has been obtained from the copyright owner.

At the present time, it is unusual for a private person to be the copyright owner of a work of firmware. Most items of firmware are considered to be compilations or other works prepared, usually by a team of people, in the course of employment, so that the copyright belongs to the publishing company. However, even if that were not the case, it would almost certainly be the publishing company who would grant any permissions for the use of their works, as they would be acting on behalf of the actual copyright owner(s). So, if you want to reproduce a piece of firmware in some way or other, your first job is to write to the publisher of the work in question explaining what you wish to use, and why, and in what way you propose to reproduce it.

Rental right

Some organizations now rent out computer programs, and there is a concern that, as computers become standard equipment in many homes, renting out programs could become a growth industry. If it becomes common practice for people to rent, rather than purchase, software, the copyright owners stand to lose the royalties they derive from sales of their works.

However, Section 66 of the 1988 Copyright, Designs and Patents Act enables the Secretary of State to introduce a computer program rental right through a Statutory Instrument approved by both the House of Lords and the House of Commons, should such a rental right be deemed necessary at some time in the future. As with other rental rights, it would be unnecessary if a licensing scheme were introduced to license the rental of computer programs.

Clause 5 of Section 66 of the 1988 Act declares that the copyright in any computer program is not infringed by renting it out to members of the public following the completion of a term of 50 years from the end of the calendar year in which "copies of it were first issued to the public in electronic form".

Your own programs

Any original programs of your own will be your copyright, and therefore it's a good idea to ensure that a phrase to that effect appears on the visual display screen when the program is initially loaded. Something like *Copyright 1989 C.U. Wynn* is quite sufficient.

During 1984, the BBC Radio 4 *Chip Shop* programme advised that, as there is no formal method of copyright registration in the UK, every time you write a computer program you should deposit your working papers and a copy of the tape or disk with your solicitor or your bank. The package should be sealed and the date of deposit verified in some way. This would not enable proof of copyright ownership to be established, but would ensure that you could prove existence of your work upon the date of deposit.

Chip Shop has also advised its listeners to be wary when discussing with other parties the possibility of getting their original programs published. A problem arises when someone betrays your confidence by suggesting he is not interested in your scheme, but later appears to produce something not dissimilar! In such an instance, you might have recourse to court action for breach of confidence, and you should seek advice from your solicitor. It's advisable to confirm all discussions and negotiations with other parties in writing, keeping copies of all such correspondence, as these documents should back up your case in court.

All computer programs that you originate enjoy copyright protection for the same period of time as any other computer-generated work. In all such programs, copyright lasts for 50 years from the end of the calendar year in which the work was created.

Computer games

Each of the comments made in this chapter regarding computer programs applies equally to computer games, bearing in mind that a computer game is, after all, nothing more than an individual type of program.

An interesting test case confirmed that copyright subsists in computer games software as if they were works of a literary nature. The case was that of Sega Enterprises Ltd *versus* Richards and another. During the hearing, the judge pointed out that copyright exists in the assembly code program of a computer game, and that the machine code program derived from it was either a reproduction or an adaptation of the copyright work. This has been confirmed by the 1988 Copyright, Designs and Patents Act.

Software piracy

Illegal copying of computer software has been estimated to cost the industry millions of pounds every year, and this high cost presumably slows down the development of new products.

With a view to pooling ideas, and to present a united front against the pirates, major commercial users and creators of software have formed the *Federation Against Software Theft* (FAST). Among its objectives, FAST is endeavouring to secure wide respect for software copyright. Some software publishers are now producing tapes or disks in such a way that they cannot be copied. Signals may be incorporated into the original programs which, when copied, have the effect of disabling computer commands. So, if you purchase a program that fails to operate properly, you could well have obtained a counterfeit. In which case, you should return it to your supplier to be exchanged for the real thing, or even better, inform the Trading Standards Department of your local authority!

Because of the high costs of development, some suppliers of specialist software insist on customers signing a special software licensing agreement before the software is supplied. Such licences state the terms on which the software is provided, and could even limit the use of particular programs to specific machines.

Actions continue against software pirates. Representatives of seven member companies of the Federation Against Software Theft, along with members of the regional crime squad and a local trading standards officer got together in 1987 to track down a Torquay company, TOS International, which was suspected of dealing in counterfeit computer software. This led to the proprietor of TOS International being charged with no less than ten offences embracing not only the copyright laws but also the Forgery and Counterfeiting Act and the Trades Description Act. He was sentenced in December 1987 to twelve months imprisonment. It later transpired that the illegal software had originated in Hong Kong, where customs officers confiscated thousands of manuals and disks and made several arrests.

In May 1988, another software pirate was prosecuted at Clacton in Essex. At this hearing, the magistrates imposed a fine of £4400 plus £100 costs in an effort to demonstrate that it is far better to stay on the right side of the law.

Sources of information

The *British Computer Society* can supply a list of computer interest books published by a variety of publishers. Write for details to the address in Appendix 2.

For educational use, particularly in junior and middle schools, the monthly journal *Junior Education* provides regular information and reviews about the very latest programs from educational publishers.

The *Church Computer Users Group* provides a useful forum for those churches and other religious organizations that make use of microcomputers. The address of their membership secretary is given in Appendix 2. Microcomputers are becoming increasingly popular as standard equipment within the Christian community. The publication *Church Computing:A Strategy* by Gareth Morgan (Jay books) will be of particular interest to those who require information on this topic.

7
Artistic works

Photography

The Copyright, Designs and Patents Act 1988 is an historical milestone in the history of photographic copyright. In this Act, the Government has classified photography alongside other works of art, and declared that the creator of a photograph is the first owner of copyright in that work. The only exception to this is that, if a photograph is taken by an employee as part of the natural course of their employment, then the employer becomes the first owner of copyright in that work, unless there is a mutual agreement to the contrary.

Owners of copyrights in photographs are at liberty to sell or assign their copyrights to other parties. As with literary, dramatic and musical works, the duration of copyright is from the time the work is created, until 50 years from the end of the calendar year in which the creator dies.

Photographers must not overlook the fact that an intended subject for a photograph may well of itself be in copyright, therefore requiring the owner's consent prior to shooting it. In some instances it is possible to purchase, for a nominal fee, a licence permitting the taking of photographs. Examples of a situation where this might apply are in certain cathedrals, major churches and similar buildings of great interest to the general public.

Technically, it may be claimed that each one of us owns our own copyright and that, therefore, nobody should actually photograph us without first obtaining our individual permission. But maybe that is stretching the point too far! It has been suggested that being included, unawares, in a snapshot constitutes an occupational hazard of being in a public place.

People who spend a lot of time being photographed, fashion models for instance, are sometimes asked to sign a form which assigns their copyright to the model agency or some other party, and grants unrestricted use of photographs. This is a practice that *may* be updated in the future, in the light of the 1988 Act.

I was once asked about the legalities of taking a photograph of an existing photograph. This is an interesting point, because unless the film is dated it may well be difficult to prove that such a copy has been produced. However, the fact is clear that unless the original is

out of copyright (i.e. the photographer died more than 50 years ago) it would be an infringement to take such a second generation picture without the appropriate permission from the copyright owner.

On the other hand, taking a new original picture of an identical scene would initiate a new original photograph!

But when does a photograph come into existence? At one time, it was deemed to be from the point in time when a negative had actually been developed. However, in our 1988 Act, the legal definition of a photograph is said to be a recording of light or other radiation on any medium on which an image is produced, or from which an image "may by any means be produced". This definition, surely, implies that the copyright is in existence even on the undeveloped film.

For reasons best known to themselves, some keen photographers have been known to take photographs of images portrayed on their television sets. It is generally assumed that they simply want photographs of their favourite stars. Well, whatever the reason, such photography has been declared as legal in the 1988 Act, which states that no infringement of copyright takes place on condition that all such photographs are retained for personal, private and domestic use.

Works of art

Artistic works include, not only photographs, but also paintings, sculptures, drawings, and so on. The term of copyright is the same as authors enjoy for their books; the work of artists is protected by copyright from the time of creation until 50 years after their decease (in Britain; for other European countries see the comments under *Period of copyright* in Chapter 1).

A special arrangement applies when the identity of an author or artist is unknown, and their work is being made available to the public (e.g. by performance, broadcast, exhibition, etc.). In such instances, the period of copyright expires 50 years from the end of the calendar year in which the work was first made available to the public. However, if during this period the identity of the author or artist comes to light, the period of copyright protection reverts to being 50 years following their death.

Whoever creates an original work of art or paints an original picture is the first owner of the copyright in that work except in certain defined cases. The artist is not the copyright owner if his work has been commissioned, and paid for, by another party. In this instance, the person or persons responsible for commissioning the work, and paying for it, becomes the copyright owner. For example, a university may commission and pay for a portrait of its Dean to be painted. Once the bursar has approved the work, accepted delivery, and handed over the agreed fee, the copyright becomes the property of the university. Copyright would subsist for 50 years from the end of the calendar year in which the artist died.

Where a work is produced during the normal course of somebody's employment, the original copyright is vested in the employer unless there exists an agreement between the employer and employee to the contrary.

The Copyright, Designs and Patents Act 1988, makes it clear that copyright in an artistic work is *not* infringed when a copy is made, or copies are issued to the public, for the purpose of advertising the sale of the work. However, in the event that any such copies are used for other purposes, including being sold or put on public exhibition, those copies are immediately deemed to be infringing copies.

Graphic art

Works of graphic art embody such items as cartoons, illustrations for books and advertisements in catalogues and magazines. Such works are copyright from the time they are created, with the period of copyright lasting for 50 years from the death of the graphic artist.

If a piece of graphic art is commissioned and paid for by another party, e.g. a company wishing to use a graphic design amongst its promotional material, then the copyright in that particular work is usually vested in the commissioning party.

Should graphic art be produced by someone as part of their terms of employment, e.g. if the artist is employed by a journal publisher specifically to illustrate articles, it is usual for the copyright to be vested in the name of that person's employer.

Bear in mind that the period of copyright extends to the end of the calendar year which falls 50 years from the death of the creator. This applies even if the copyright has been assigned to another party, or is the property of a commercial company, having been produced by the creator as part of their contract of employment. To ensure that there can be no doubt as to whether or not a work is still enjoying copyright protection, it is as well to indicate the situation by incorporating, perhaps in small print in one corner, a phrase similar to: © 1992 Graphitus Plc. Drawn by Neil Downe, July 1992.

'Copyright free' artwork

Producers of amateur magazines, such as the newsletters of local clubs, societies and churches, are always on the lookout for graphic artwork that may be used freely in order to enhance the image of their production.

Certain manufacturers of 'rub-down' lettering sheets, such as Letraset Ltd, include among their range some sheets of graphic illustrations that may be used without further permission. It is probable that any charges applicable are included in the purchase price of the sheets of artwork.

Other commercial companies have produced books of what is described as *copyright free* artwork. In practice, it is generally only free for use in amateur productions; permission is often required for commercial use. Details are given, as appropriate, within each collection of ready-to-use artwork.

Typefaces

Although typeface designs attract an artistic copyright, that copyright is not infringed when a typeface is utilized during the normal course of typing, composing a text, typesetting or printing.

Architectural designs and buildings

For the purposes of copyright legislation, architectural designs and buildings are classified under the general heading of artistic works. So it will be seen that the creator (usually the architect) of such drawings and features is usually the first owner of copyright in any such work; sometimes it may be the architect's employers.

Anything done for the sole purpose of reconstructing a building does not infringe copyright, either in the building itself, or in any drawings or plans relevant to the building. This statement *hints* that, should it be necessary to reconstruct any given building, for any reason, it would be quite permissible to have the original plans altered, without infringing the copyright owned by the original architect. In practice, it is not all that common for a building to require reconstructing during the term of original copyright.

Should a model (scale model or otherwise) of a building be permanently situated in a public place, or sited within premises open to the public, then the copyright in that building is not infringed by anybody producing a graphic work to represent the building, taking a photograph of it, filming it, or even broadcasting a visual image of it. Further, it should be noted that copyright is not infringed should any of the aforementioned items be issued to the public.

It was noted in Chapter 1 that an author has the moral right to demand to be identified as such in a prominent place on their book. This *right of paternity* is in fact extended to the creators of virtually all copyright works. So, when the creator is the architect of a building, the 1988 Act (section 77, clause 5) provides them with the legal right to insist on their name being displayed in some way on the building at the time it is constructed. However, if more than one building is to be produced to an identical plan, e.g. a street of similar houses, then the architect may insist only on being identified on the first to be built.

If the building, or a model of the building, or a sculpture, is photographed or otherwise depicted graphically so that copies can be supplied to the general public, the architect or sculptor has the right to be identified on each and every such copy.

Design right

As copyright is a property right of intellectual innovation, so design right is a property right which subsists in an original design of any aspect of the shape or configuration of the whole, or part, of an article. Suppose you come up with a design to produce an original garment to be manufactured out of used phone cards. You produce a blueprint along with a prototype in order to promote your design to prospective manufacturers. You own the right – the design right – in that original design of yours.

It's important to emphasize that design right can only subsist in genuinely original designs that have been recorded in a design document, or where an article has been produced, such as a scale model, in strict accordance with the design. Your design, for example, could not be considered original if your colleagues were producing skirts out of old phone cards at the same time that you were working on your effort.

The designer is the first owner of a design right. In the case of a computer-generated design, the designer is the person who made the necessary arrangements to enable the design to be created. Exceptionally, if a design is created by somebody during the normal course of their employment, the employer becomes the first owner of that design right unless there is any special agreement to the contrary. If a design is created as a result of a commission, then the person who commissioned it has the honour of being the first owner of the design right.

Owners of design rights are quite at liberty to sell, or assign, their design rights to other people or companies. Whenever such a deal is transacted, it is advisable for the respective parties to confirm their agreements in writing, either by a simple exchange of letters in which the terms agreed are set out clearly, or through a deed of contract preferably, though not necessarily, prepared by a solicitor.

I was once asked whether a model of a proposed building, prepared by an architect, attracted copyright as an artistic work, or design right as a design. The 1988 legislation indicates that such a model for a building acquires artistic copyright for its creator, the architect. Its copyright subsists until the end of the calendar year that comes round 50 years after the death of the architect.

On the other hand, the creator of a design for, say, a special box in which to package toy bricks, or an original design for a telephone, could claim ownership of the *design right* in the original *design*.

Term of design right

It is sometimes assumed that design right is operative for a similar period to that of other artistic works. However, the duration of design right is actually rather shorter than that enjoyed by artistic copyright holders.

Design right expires 15 years from the end of the calendar year in which the design was first recorded in a design document, or an article is manufactured to the design, whichever may have been undertaken first. *However*, if articles to the design are made available for sale or for hire within five years from the time of first recording or first making of an article, the design right expires ten years from the end of the calendar year in which the availability for sale or hire was first introduced.

Unlike copyright in, say, a painted oil masterpiece, it is possible to register your design at the Patents Office. You should then include in your design document the symbol ® which indicates that yours is a registered design. If for any reason your application to register your design is turned down, do check with the Patents Office the reason for their rejection. It could be that your design does not qualify for design right protection, in which case it will qualify for general copyright protection as an artistic work.

Design right in garments

Fashion creators, and in fact all garment designers, produce their instructions to clothing factories in the form of drawings known as *patterns*. Patterns are fully protected in copyright legislation through the design right. This is especially important when you consider how easy it is these days to imitate, say, someone else's dress designs or shirt patterns.

As with audiovisual copyrights, piracy is intruding in the clothing industries, with low-cost inferior quality garments that 'look' like the original creations. The Commission of the European Communities noted this unfortunate fact, and in its 1988 Copyright Green Paper indicated that such illicit manufacturing practices weakened the market for all members of the European Economic Community. The Commission hope that, having been recognized, the problem will not mushroom.

DACS Copyright Clearance Service

Many commercial bodies, notably publishing houses, are increasingly wishing to use reproductions of works of art in their leaflets, booklets and books. However, they have often found it difficult to trace the name and address of an artist or sculptor or their estate or other copyright owner. It has often been possible to obtain permission at an art gallery to shoot a transparency of a picture, but this only provides access to the work; before a masterpiece can be photographed, the additional permission of the actual copyright owner is required.

Responding positively to the problem, the Design and Artists Copyright Society introduced its *DACS Copyright Clearance Service*. In effect, this service obtains all of the necessary permissions on your behalf, and is highly convenient for publishers and others who may wish to use more than one artist's work, as there is.only one address to deal with. As with other copyright societies, the Design and Artists Copyright Society can act only on behalf of its members, but the majority of artists, sculptors and designers are probably in membership.

Using the service is not complicated. Simply write to the society (address in Appendix 2), telephone it on 01–247 1650, or fax it on 01–377 5855, and ask for a copyright clearance request form. Don't forget to provide the society with your full name and postal address! The form calls for essential basic information, such as the title of the work you wish to use, the artist's name, whether your printing will be in full colour or black and white, etc. When completed, you return the form to DACS who will obtain the permission(s) on your behalf, issue you with a licence, a legal agreement, the copyright byline, details of any special conditions, etc. It will also invoice you for all permissions requested at any one time. As with other copyright requests, always apply to DACS as far in advance as possible. Six weeks minimum notice is preferred.

Patents and trade marks

In essence, a patent in an invention, or a registered trade mark, is rather like an up-market form of copyright protection. Suppose you hit upon an idea for a revolutionary alarm clock. Once you have written down your recipe and produced the necessary drawings, your instructions are your copyright property. But as there is no legal copyright in ideas, you can protect your achievement from exploitation by taking out a patent registration in respect of your invention.

Inventions may be registered at HM Patents Office, High Holborn, London. However, registration is a lengthy process, and therefore it is now common practice to instruct a patent agent to apply for registration on your behalf. Some agencies describe themselves as *European patent agents* to reflect the fact that they act for clients in more than one EEC country. Patent agents must be registered as such, and local agents are often listed in commercial telephone directories, such as *Yellow Pages*.

Having applied for patent registration, you may publish the words "patent pending" on your invention, and any sales literature pertinent to it, until you receive either a rejection or a patent number.

Sometimes you may come across a firm describing itself as *patent attorney* or *European patent attorney*. These are terms used by patent solicitors.

Should you design a special logo, perhaps for your company or one of its products, you may consider it wise to register the same as an official trade mark. The symbol ⓜ printed in the vicinity of your logo announces that your motif is a registered trade mark.

Trade marks are also registered at HM Patents Office but, again, it is becoming accepted practice to appoint a trade mark agent to take out the registration on your behalf.

8
Live performance

Those who stage a theatrical style performance of any work, be it a dramatic or musical work, a reading or recitation of some literary work, or even the performance of a presentation such as a variety act or a pop concert, may claim a *performance right* in their original 'live' presentation. Note that this is an entirely separate and distinct right from any copyright of the actual work performed. This performance right requires that the consent of individual performers is obtained for the exploitation of any or all of their performances.

A further consequence is that it is necessary to obtain prior permission from performers to make any record or broadcast any performance. A performer may enter into an exclusive recording contract with another person or company to make recordings with a view to commercial sales. Once such an agreement is concluded, all other persons (as well as the performer) would be excluded from making recordings for commercial exploitation.

Both of the above rights subsist for a period of 50 years from the end of the calendar year in which a performance takes place. Unlike many other rights, these rights are not assignable or transmissible, with the exception of the terms of an exclusive recording contract, although they may be transferred on death by means of a bequest.

Exceptionally, there is no legal requirement to obtain permission from a performer to make a recording of their performance provided it is strictly for private and domestic use. Such a recording is described in section 180 of the 1988 Act as a 'film or sound recording'.

Section 5 of the Act defines *film* as any medium of recording that allows a 'moving image' to be produced. This clearly includes video recording.

Previously, under the Performers' Protection Acts of 1958, 1963 and 1972, it was generally reckoned that individual permissions from every performer at an event were required even for private and domestic audio and video recording, and for the shooting of amateur cine films. It is apparent, therefore, that the Copyright, Designs and Patents Act 1988 has opened the way for private individuals whose desire is nothing more than to have a sound or visual souvenir of their visit to the theatre or concert hall. Presumably it was as a

consequence of the aforementioned Performers' Protection Acts, now repealed, that most theatres introduced regulations prohibiting photography and recording of performances. Only time will tell if these rules will be dropped in the light of current legislation.

Unfortunately, the 1988 Act does not specifically mention the taking of photographs. Commonsense surely would dictate that, as it is not an offence to make recordings of performers for private and domestic use, this privilege should be extended to cover still, as well as movie, photography. However, as it's always better to be safe than sorry, photographers would be well advised to seek permission before they commence snapping. There may be some other good reason why flashlight photography is not allowed.

By ensuring that all types of performances are included in the 1988 Act, the Government has respected the work of such people as variety artistes (for example) who do not normally put on a live performance of a published work such as a play or musical. Nevertheless, they do usually perform a work that involves considerable talent and expertise, such as juggling or acrobatics.

If you wish to make a recording or broadcast of the performance, or take photographs of a work that is still in copyright for wider use than privately at home, you will need, in addition to the performers' consent, to seek permission from the copyright owner of that actual work. In case of doubt, write to the publishers of that work.

Performing licence

There is also the matter of a performing licence to be taken into account. If you are involved with a group planning to put on a public performance of a work that is currently still in copyright, you will almost certainly require such a licence. Licences are normally supplied by the Performing Right Society on behalf of the publishers of musical works. In some instances, an address to write to for a performing licence is given on the back of the title page of the published edition.

For professional use, licences are always required. However, for amateur productions such as school plays or church music group presentations where no charge is being made for admission, you may discover that a licence to perform is not necessary. Where a charge is being levied at the door, even if proceeds are going to your favourite charity, you will almost certainly need a performing licence. But please don't risk *thinking* that you do not need such a licence; take the trouble to write to the publishers or to the PRS first to find out.

The cost of a performing licence for amateur performances, whether or not they are in aid of charitable causes, is nearly always considerably less than that charged for more professional performances. It is almost certainly cheaper than the cost that might be incurred if the copyright owner discovers, at some later date, that you failed to obtain a licence in respect of your performance.

The Performing Right Society

If the organization you belong to frequently holds events using live performers or music, you may find it worth your while to drop a line to the Performing Right Society (address in Appendix 2) explaining what you get up to. It may be that it can be of assistance to you, by offering you a service that will save you a lot of time and expense. For example, some village halls that regularly hold dances have been able to take out a PRS licence, renewable on an annual basis, covering their premises in respect of singing and music.

If you are in any doubt as to whether or not your particular use of 'live' activities might be enough to warrant a scheme from the Performing Right Society, contact it anyway. Its advice is offered freely, and it has a reputation for being most helpful. In certain instances, PRS has issued *permits* (rather than licences) covering either a particular repertoire or designated specific works. These permits cover either one performance or a short series of performances, depending on the individual requirements of the organization concerned.

The society is an association of composers, authors and publishers of musical works, so a PRS licence is required in respect of any public performance of copyright music, whether the performance is live or by other means, such as a juke box or a background music tape. This has the far-reaching effect that places other than theatres and halls often require a PRS licence, e.g. ships, aircraft, bingo halls, shops, factories and hotels, to name but a few!

As PRS concerns itself only with performances of a musical nature, it has been known for an amateur dramatic society not to apply for a PRS licence when planning to put on a play. However, what must be taken into account is that background music is frequently played immediately before the production commences, in order to help the arriving audience settle down in a relaxed and receptive manner. There will probably be more during the interval, and possibly again while the theatre is emptying. Do review your plans extremely carefully, and do not forget that if you make use of recorded music, a licence is usually also necessary from Phonographic Performance in respect of the actual recording.

Arrangements and adaptations

Copyright automatically exists in any original musical or literary work. Composers own the copyright in their own work unless they assign it to another party. When musical works are published composers sometimes assign the copyright to their publishers as part of the deal.

Where composers do own the copyright in a particular work and they have reason to think it is being infringed, they can take action by claiming for damages, or obtain an injunction to prevent further use of the work without their express permission.

It should be noted that there is no copyright in a title or idea, although action might be taken if a copyright owner had reason to believe that their work was being passed off by others as their own.

One of the acts restricted through copyright legislation is the adaptation of a work of literary, dramatic or musical nature. Perhaps the most common types of copyright properties to attract adaptation are computer programs and musical works; the latter being a giant magnet attracting all manner of arrangements. Thus arrangers should obtain permission from the owners of musical copyrights before commencing work on their arrangements or adaptations. Generally speaking, the owners or controllers of music copyrights rarely object to granting permission for arrangements being made, especially since they and the composers involved should, at least in theory, benefit in that new arrangements encourage further performances!

It could probably be argued that a person who conjures up an original arrangement of, say, a song, owns the copyright in that *arrangement*. But irrespective of whether or not that argument holds water, the arranger certainly needs authority from the owner of the original work to both arrange and use that arrangement (see page 19).

Public houses

Frequent visitors to public houses, hotels, motels, and similar establishments will have observed the increasing popularity of a blue and white 'PRS' sign at those places that include live performances of music among their attractions. The sign indicates that the establishment displaying it has a licence from the Performing Right Society in respect of such live performances.

The *Public House Licence* came about as a result of negotiations between the Performing Right Society and the National Union of Licensed Victuallers (also representing the Scottish Licensed Trade Association).

At the time of going to press, where a public house spends £5000 or more a year on live music, a royalty is levied at the rate of 6 per cent of the total expenditure. For public houses whose relevant costs are less than this, or for discos, the royalty rate comes in line with that paid by hotels and restaurants. This is based on the capacity of the room in which an event takes place as determined for the fire regulations. It is currently £3.20 for the first 100 persons and 80p for each subsequent 25 persons. Current details are available direct from the Performing Right Society, whose address is listed in Appendix 2.

Peter Pan

Although the copyright in respect of *Peter Pan* by Sir J M Barrie expired on 31 December 1987, the 1988 Act makes special provision in clause 301 for royalties in respect of this work to be paid perpetually for the benefit of the Hospital for Sick Children, Great Ormond Street, London. Such royalties have to be paid in respect of all public performances, broadcasting, cable diffusion and commercial publishing.

If you are involved with an amateur dramatic group, including school or church organizations, and your club is considering putting on a performance of *Peter Pan*, note that the 1988 Act confers the royalties to the Hospital for Sick Children in respect of *all* public performances, either straight or adaptations. It is quite plain that even performances in aid of charities, or to boost your own funds, come under this umbrella. As a general guide, most amateur groups donate to the Hospital's trustees about ten per cent of the income derived from sales of tickets and programmes. Your club might consider putting on a performance and donating all the takings; the trustees are always appreciative of such initiatives.

This exceptional arrangement is of particular historical interest as it is probably the only piece of copyright legislation to date to confer an everlasting arrangement, which can only be terminated or amended by a change in the British law. It has come about as a result of representations on behalf of the hospital. When his classic children's play was first produced in 1904, and subsequently published in book form in 1911, Sir James Barrie directed that all his royalties should go to Great Ormond Street. Over the years, the hospital has received a large and continuing income from the book and theatrical productions. This income was likely to be cut off, without the special provision that has now been made.

Appendix 1
Copyright notices ————————————

Examples of copyright notices that may be found printed in books

Example 1 General

All rights reserved. No part of this book may be reproduced, stored in a retrieval system or transmitted in any form or by any means, electronic, electrostatic, mechanical, photocopying, recording or otherwise without permission in writing from the publishers.

Example 2 General

All rights reserved. No reproduction, copy or transmission of this publication may be made without prior written permission.

No paragraph of this publication may be reproduced, copied or transmitted, save with written permission or in accordance with the provisions of the Copyright, Designs and Patents Act 1988, or under the terms of any licence permitting limited copying issued by the Copyright Licensing Agency.

Any person who does any unauthorized act in relation to this publication may be liable to criminal prosecution and civil claims for damages.

Example 3 CLA licence excluded title

All rights reserved. No reproduction, copy or transmission of this publication may be made without written permission.

No paragraph of this publication may be reproduced, copied or transmitted, save with written permission or in accordance with the provisions of the Copyright, Designs and Patents Act 1988.

Any person who does any unauthorized act in relation to this publication may be liable to criminal prosecution and civil claims for damages.
WARNING
This publication is *not* part of the copyright licensing scheme run by the Copyright Licensing Agency and may *not* be photographed or mechanically copied in any other way, without prior written permission from the publisher.

Example 4 Book covered by CMA licence

All rights reserved. No part of this publication may be reproduced, stored in a retrieval system, or transmitted, in any form or by any means, electronic, mechanical, photocopying, recording or otherwise, without the prior permission in writing of the publisher.

Certain items included in this book remain the copyright of individual authors and/or composers, as stated against the relevant items. Application to reproduce these items should be sought via the publisher.

The contents of this book are covered by the provisions of the Christian Music Association licence, but do not fall within the terms of any blanket copyright provisions that may be granted by any other publisher or organization.

Example 5 Black line masters

All rights reserved. No reproduction, copy or transmission of this publication may be made without written permission, except under the terms set out on page 00.*

No paragraph of this publication may be produced, copied or transmitted, save with written permission or in accordance with the provisions of the Copyright, Designs and Patents Act 1988, or under the terms of any licence permitting limited copying issued by the Copyright Licensing Agency.

Any person who does any unauthorized act in relation to this publication may be liable to criminal prosecution and civil claims for damages.

Further note on page 00 relating to the section of the book which may be copied:
This publication is copyright, but teachers are free to reproduce by any method without fee or prior permission the pages in this section, provided that the number of copies made does not exceed the amount required in their school. For copying in any other circumstances (e.g. other than a school) prior written permission must be obtained from the publisher, and a fee may be payable.

Example 6 Spirit duplicator masters

This publication is copyright, but teachers are free to reproduce it using the masters provided by the spirit duplicator process *only*. Application must be made to the publisher for permission to copy by persons other than teachers, and/or for permission to copy by any other process.

Examples of copyright notices that may be found on audio and/or video recordings

Example 1 Audio

All rights of the record producer and of the owner of the work reproduced reserved. Copying, public performance and broadcasting of this record prohibited.

Example 2 Audio

Copyright recording: all rights of the publisher and owner of this recording reserved. Copying/re-recording/broadcasting in part or whole prohibited without a licence.

Example 3 Video

Warning: this video cassette including its soundtrack is protected by copyright. This video cassette may be used to show the motion picture programme only in private homes to which the general public is not invited and/or to which an entrance fee is not charged. Any other unauthorized manner of exhibition and broadcast, public performance, diffusion, editing, copying, reselling, and hiring in whole or in part is prohibited. This prohibition may be enforced by legal action.

Example 4 Video

The film contained in this video cassette is fully protected by copyright and is restricted to private home viewing only. Any other manner of exhibition and any broadcast, public performance, diffusion, copying, re-selling or editing constitutes an infringement of copyright unless the previous written consent of the copyright owner hereto has been obtained. Any infringement of this copyright will be subject to prosecution.

Appendix 2
Organizations

American Library Association
50 East Huron Street, Chicago, Illinois 60611, USA

Association of Illustrators
1 Colville Place, London W1P 1HN

Association of Independent Producers
17 Great Pulteney Street, London W1R 3DG

Association of Learned & Professional Society Publishers
Sentosa, Hill Road, Fairlight, Hastings, East Sussex TN35 4AE

Australian Copyright Council
22 Alfred Street, Milsons Point, New South Wales 2061, Australia

BBC Copyright Department
Broadcasting House, Portland Place, London W1A 1AA

British Academy of Songwriters, Composers and Authors
34 Hanway Street, London W1P 9DE

British Copyright Council
29 Berners Street, London W1P 4AA

British Computer Society
13 Mansfield Street, London, W1M OBP

British Equity
8 Harley Street, London W1N 2AB

British Film Institute
21 Stephen Street, London W1P 1PL

British Library Copyright Receipt Office
2 Sheraton Street, London W1V 4BH

British Phonographic Industry
Roxburghe House, 273 Regent Street, London W1R 8BN

British Videogram Association
22 Poland Street, London W1V 3DD

Cable Television Association
50 Frith Street, London W1V 5TE

Campaign against Book Piracy
19 Bedford Square, London WC1B 3HJ

Channel Four TV Recording Licence Department
Guild Licensing, 6 Royce Road, Peterborough PE1 5YB

Chartered Society of Designers
29 Bedford Square, London WC1 3EG

Christian Music Association
Glyndley Manor, Stone Cross, Pevensey, East Sussex BN24 5BS

Church Computer Users Group
30 The Crescent, Solihull, West Midlands B91 1JR

Commonwealth Secretariat
Marlborough House, Pall Mall, London SW1Y 5HX

Composers' Guild of Great Britain
34 Hanway Street, London W1P 9DE

Copyright Clearance Center
27 Congress Street, Salem, Massachusetts 01970, USA

Copyright Licensing Agency
33–34 Alfred Place, London WC1E 7DP

Design and Artists Copyright Society
St Mary's Clergy House, 2 Whitechurch Lane, London E1 7QR

Educational Publishers Council
19 Bedford Square, London WC1B 3HJ

Federation Against Software Theft
7 Victory Business Centre, Worton Road, Isleworth TW7 6ER

Guild Learning
Guild House, Oundle Road, Peterborough PE2 9PZ

Independent Broadcasting Authority
70 Brompton Road, London SW3 1EY

Independent Film, Video and Photography Association
79 Wardour Street, London W1V 3PH

Independent Publishers Guild
147 Gloucester Terrace, London W2 6DX

Independent Television Association
Knighton House, 56 Mortimer Street, London W1N 8AN

International Federation of Producers of Phonograms and Videograms
IFPI Secretariat, 54 Regent Street, London W1R 5PJ

International Federation of Reproductive Rights Organizations
27 Congress Street, Salem, Massachusetts 01970, USA

International Publishers' Association
Avenue de Miremont 3, 1206 Geneva, Switzerland

International Songwriters' Association
22 Sullane Crescent, Raheen Heights, Limerick, Ireland

Irish Book Publishers' Association
65 Middle Abbey Street, Dublin 1, Ireland

Library Association
7 Ridgmount Street, London WC1E 7AE

London Weekend Television
South Bank, London SE1 9LT

Mechanical-Copyright Protection Society
Elgar House, 41 Streatham High Road, London SW16 1ER

Music Publishers' Association
7th Floor Kingsway House, 103 Kingsway, London WC2B 6QX

Musicians' Union
60 Clapham Road, London SW9 0JJ

National Council for Educational Technology
3 Devonshire Street, London W1N 2BA

Patent Office
Industrial Property and Copyright Dept, Room 1504, State House, 66 High Holborn, London WC1R 4TP

Performing Right Society
29–33 Berners Street, London W1P 4AA

Periodical Publishers Association
Imperial House, Kingsway, London WC2B 6UN

Phonographic Performance Ltd
Ganton House, 14 Ganton Street, London W1V 1LB

Poetry Society
21 Earls Court Square, London SW5 9BY

Public Lending Right Registrar
Bayheath House, Prince Regent Street, Stockton-on-Tees TS18 1DF

Publishers Association
19 Bedford Square, London WC1B 3HJ

Publishers Licensing Society
33–34 Alfred Place, London WC1E 7DP

Scottish Publishers Association
25a South West Thistle Street Lane, Edinburgh EH2 1EW

A T Smail
100 Euston Street, London NW1 2HQ

Society of Authors
84 Drayton Gardens, London SW10 9SB

Songwriters' Guild of Great Britain
148 Charing Cross Road, London WC2H 0LB

Stationers' Hall Copyright Registry
Ave Maria Lane, London EC4M 7DD

UNESCO International Copyright Information Centre
7 Place de Fontenoy, 75700 Paris, France

United Kingdom Anti-Piracy Group
19 Bedford Square, London WC1B 3HJ

Video Copyright Protection Society
Visnews House, Cumberland Avenue, London NW10 7EH

Visual Artists Rights Society
108 Old Brompton Road, London SW7 3RA

World Intellectual Property Organization
34 Chemin des Colombettes, 1211 Geneva 20, Switzerland

Writers' Guild of Great Britain
430 Edgware Road, London W2 1EH

Appendix 3
Recorded Music Libraries _____

The organizations in this list maintain audio music libraries, consisting of music recorded onto disc and/or tape. Their material is available for re-recording upon payment of appropriate fees.

Amphonic Music Ltd
Kerchesters, Waterhouse Lane, Kingswood, Surrey KT20 6HT

April Orchestra Library
c/o CBS Songs Ltd, 3–5 Rathbone Place, London W1P 1DA

Atmosphere Music Library
6–10 Lexington Street, London W1R 3HS

Beadle Music Ltd
Suite D, The Priory, Haywards Heath, West Sussex RH16 4DG

Boosey and Hawkes Music Publishers Ltd
295 Regent Street, London W1A 1BR

Bosworth and Co Ltd
14/18 Heddon Street, Regent Street, London W1R 8DP

Bruton Music
11 Greek Street, London W1V 5LE

BTW Music Ltd
125 Myddleton Road, Wood Green, London N22 4NG

Chandos Music Ltd
93 Shepperton Road, London NW1 3DF

Chappell Music Ltd
129 Park Street, London W1Y 3FA

De Wolfe Ltd
80/82 Wardour Street, London W1V 3LF

Image Music Ltd
1st Floor, Unit 3, King Street, London N2 8DY

Iota Music
62 Weald Drive, Furnace Green, Crawley, West Sussex RH10 6PX

Jammy Music Publishers Ltd
Inchbank House, 957 Dumbarton Road, Glasgow G14 9UF

Josef Weinberger Ltd
10–16 Rathbone Street, London W1P 2BJ

J R B Music
170 Coxley View, Netherton, Wakefield, W. Yorkshire WF4 4NE

Just Pleasure Music
Fruit Farm House, Foxton, Cambs CB2 6RT

KMP Music Group
21 Denmark Street, London WC2H 0NE

Lemmel Music Ltd
Cray Avenue, Orpington, Kent BR5 3PA

Match Music Library
Suite 1A, Lansdowne House, Landsdowne Road, London W11 3LP

Montparnasse 2000
c/o Belwin Mills Music Ltd, 250 Purley Way, Croydon CR9 4QD

Mood-Spectrum Music Publishers
22 High Street, Hampton Hill, Middlesex TW12 1PD

Mozart Edition (GB) Ltd
Suite E, 2nd Floor, Greenhill House, 90/93 Cowcross Street,
London EC1M 6BH

Music Ltd
Whistlers Wood, The Ridge, Woldingham, Surrey CR3 7AN

Music House (International) Ltd
5 Newburgh Street, London W1V 1LH

Music Masters Ltd
28 St Lawrence Drive, Eastcote, Middlesex HA5 2RU

Photoplay Music Ltd
Flat 10, 73 Portland Place, London W1N 3AL

Q Music Ltd
1487 Melton Road, Queniborough, Leics LE7 8FP

Red Bus Music Library
34 Salisbury Street, London NW8 8QE

Ritz Music
No 8, 21 Fitzjohn Avenue, London NW3 5JY

Shepherds Bush Library Music
15A Woodstock Grove, London W12 8LE

Southern Library of Recorded Music
8 Denmark Street, London WC2 8LT

Studio G
Ridgeway House, Gt Brington, Northhampton NN7 4JA

Studio Music Company
77–79 Dudden Lane, London NW10 1BD

Terrific Music
63 Charlotte Street, London W1P 1LA

Twist And Shout Music
1st–2nd Floors, 12 Kingdon Road, West Hampstead,
London NW6 1PH

Vivo Music Ltd
Barley Break, Mouleford-on-Thames, Wellingford, Berks OX10 9JD

Appendix 4
CLA–excluded works

The following books, periodicals and journals are *excluded* from the CLA licence and permission must be obtained direct from the publisher before copying *any* of them, even by those holding a CLA licence.

Chemical Abstracts Service
Chemical & Engineering News
Chemtech

American Chemical Society

All publications

Anbar Publications Ltd

All publications

The Association of Commonwealth Universities

All periodicals and journals
(*not* books)
Software documentation
Teachers notes, pupils
pamphlets and Radiovision
notes

BBC Publications

All publications

BBP Holdings Plc

All academic, professional
and reference titles: Blackie,
International Textbook Company,
Leonard Hill, Surrey University
Press

Blackie & Son Ltd

Alfred Hitchcock anthologies
(Davis Publications)
A Man (Oriana Fallaci)

The Bodley Head Ltd

All publications

British Industrial Publicity
Overseas

The British Journal of Radiology

British Institute of Radiology

All publications	British Standards Institution
All publications	British Telecom Plc
Running your own Restaurant (J H Johnson)	Century Hutchinson Ltd
All Berlitz titles	Charles Letts & Company Ltd
All works by Iris Origo	Chatto & Windus
All publications	Checkmate Publications Ltd
All publications	The Conde Naste Publications Ltd
All publications	Conway Maritime Press
The Rousing of the Scottish Working Class (James Young)	Croom Helm Ltd
All works by Dylan Thomas	J M Dent & Sons Ltd
First Aid Manual (British Red Cross Society) Caring for the Sick (St John's Ambulance Assoc., St Andrew's Ambulance Assoc.)	Dorling Kindersley Ltd
State & Capital: A Marxist Debate (J Holloway & S Picciott)	Edward Arnold
All publications	Encounter Ltd
All publications	Eyre & Spottiswoode
All publications	Encyclopaedia Britannica
Card Tricks without Skill (Paul Clive) All works by P A Downie Dictionary of British Miniature Painters Samuel Cooper (Daphne Foskett) London Goldsmiths & Rococo Silver (Arthur Grimwade)	Faber and Faber Ltd
Money Management Resident Abroad IC Stockmarket Letter Financial Adviser The Banker (Investors Chronicle)	FT Business Information Ltd

All publications	Gordon & Breach Science Publishers Ltd
The Fairburn System of Visual Reform (T Fairburn)	Graphic Books International Ltd
Creative Form Drawing Vol 1 (R Kutzli)	Hawthorn Press
All publications	Hertis
HLL French 1 Exercise Book HLL German 1 Exercise Book (Baxter, Dale, Roberts, Fischer, Grote, Hayward)	HLL Publications
All publications	Hobsons Publishing Plc
All publications	Independent Television Publications Ltd
The Loss Prevention Bulletin	The Institution of Chemical Engineers
Teeline Magazine	Jazz Journal Ltd
All publications	The Lancet Ltd
All publications	Learning Development Aids
All publications	Library Association (Branches & Groups)
All publications	Library Association Publishing
All publications	Link House Publications Plc
Illustrated Handbook in Local Anaesthesia (Ejnar Eriksson) Pathology of the Foetus and the Infant (E L Potter & J M Craig) Modern Hospital: International Planning Practices (Ervin Putsep) A Back Pain Bibliography (Barry Wyke)	Lloyd-Luke (Medical Books)
All publications	LWWF
Know Your Training Films (H Johannsen)	Management Update Ltd
All publications	Marcham Manor Press

The Downwave (R C Beckman)	Milestone Publications
The 'Bible Story' series 'Getting to Know About' series 'Our Friends' series	National Christian Education Council
All publications	NATFHE Library Section
All publications	New Opportunity Press
Lexicon Crosswords (D F Stapleton) Beginners' Crosswords First Dictionary Boxwords (W D Wright)	James Nisbet
All publications	Online Publications
All publications	G J Palmer & Sons Ltd
All publications	Personnel Publications Ltd
All publications	Philograph Publications Ltd
All publications	Phonic Blend Systems Ltd
All publications	Pitmans Books Ltd (Periodicals Div)
All publications	The Plessey Company Plc
All publications	The Reader's Digest Association Ltd
All publications	Reed Business Publishing Developments
In His Presence (Denis E Taylor)	Religious and Moral Education Press
Detection and Classification of Ice (E Lewis, B Currie & S Haykin)	Research Studies Press Ltd
Clinical Radiology	Royal College of Radiologists
All publications	Royal Meteorological Society
'Journeys in Reading' series	Schofield & Sims Ltd
Bax (L Foreman) Isle of Cats (G Hoffnung & J Symonds)	Scolar Press
All publications	Scottish Library Association

All song books	Scripture Union Publishing
Resource Allocation in British Universities (M Shatrock & G Rigby)	SRHE
All publications	Sphere Books (Simon & Schuster)
All publications	Sphere Books (New American Library)
New Statesman	The Statesman & Nation Publishing Co Ltd
'Sycamore Leaves' series (Alan McWhirr)	Sycamore Press Ltd
All publications	D C Thompson & Co Ltd
The Legal Environment of the Business World (Robert Buchanan)	Stanley Thornes
All publications	The Times Supplements Ltd
'Import Reports' series	Trade Research Publications
Perspectives and Problems (D Kerby) Commerce in Everyday Life Modern Office Practice (C E Tomalin)	University Tutorial Press
Case Problems in Marketing (Kenneth Simmonds)	Van Nostrand Reinhold
Studies of the Warburg Institute Vol 31–37	The Warburg Institute
Computer Project Management (Bentley) Dictionary of Minicomputing & Microcomputing (Burton) Dictionary of Computing and Data Communication (Gallard) Atlas of Cancer Mortality (Gardner) Atlas of Mortality from Selected Diseases (Gardner) Data Compression – Techniques and Applications (Herd) GPSS Fostran (Schmidt)	John Wiley & Sons Ltd

Appendix 5
CMA copyright licence scheme _____

Copyright owners and music publishers

Agape
Bug and Bear Music
C A Music
Canaanland Music
Candle Company
Celebration
Chancel Music
Christian Music Ministries
Dandy Music
Dawn Treader Music
Dayspring Music
Lyn DeShazo
Ears and Eyes Publishing
Ward L Ellis
Fairhill Music
First Monday Music
H T Fitsimonds Co
Fred Bock Music Co
Daniel Gardner
Garpax Music
Gentry Publications
Glory Alleluia Music
Stuart K Hine
Home Sweet Home Music
Hope Publishing Co
Hosanna! Music
Jaw Music

Journey Music
Jubilate Hymns Ltd
Kenwood Music
Latter Rain Music
Peter Lawry
Lexicon/Crouch Music
Lexicon Music Inc
Libris Music
Lillenas Pub Co
Luminar Music
Maranatha! Music
Mercy Publishing
Mike & Claire McIntosh
Monk and Tid Music
Jenny Jenny (Powerpack)
Mustard Seed Music
New Branch Music
New Song Ministries
Norman Clayton Publishing Co
North Park Music
Promiseland Music
Raymond A Hoffman Co
Restoration Music
Sacred Songs
Sandy Music
Scripture in Song
Sea Dream Music

Somerset Press
Sound III Inc
Springtide Music
St Paul's Outreach Trust
Steve & Sue Steffy
Straightway Music
Wes Sutton
Tabernacle Publishing Co
Tempo Music Publications

Thankyou Music
The Masters Collection
The Rodeheaver Company
Vision Records Music
Ward Ellis
Word and Music
Word Music Inc
Word Music (UK)
Zionsong

Licensed publications and songbooks

Harvestime

Enter His Gates
Enthroned on High
King of Kings and Lord of Lords
Let Praises Ring
Let Your Spirit Rise
Make a Joyful Noise
Much Much Higher
Sing Praises unto God
Worthy is the Lamb
We are Called

Hodder & Stoughton

Carols for Today
Church Family Worship
Cry Hosanna
Fresh Sounds
Hymns for Today's Church
If my People
Sound of Living Waters
Songifts

Kingsway Publications

Dave Bilbrough Songbooks
1 & 2
Build your Church & Heal
This Land
Graham Kendrick Songbooks
1 & 2

Let the Righteous Be Glad
Make Way
New Songs 1 & 2
Passion – Adrian Snell
Power Praise
Psalm Praise
Reconciled
Scripture in Song Books 1 & 2
Sing a New Psalm
Songs of Fellowship
Songs of the Vineyard Vol 1
The Servant King
Voice to the Nation
We Declare your Majesty
Worship the King
Youth Praise

Marshall Pickering

Carol Praise
Junior Praise
Mission Praise 1 & 2

Scripture Union

Praise God Together
Sing to God
Jesus Praise

Spring Harvest

Lights to the World

This is your God
Truth and Justice

Word Music (UK)

Alpha and Omega – Adrian Snell
All Things New
Animals and Other Things
Ants' Hillvania
Awaken your Power
Bullfrogs and Butterflies
Burst into Song
If my People
Kids Praise Vols 1–6
Make a Joyful Noise
Music Machine Parts 1 & 2

Nathaniel the Grublet
Psalty's Christmas Calamity
Reign in Me – Chris Bowater
Rest in my Love – Marilyn Baker
Simply the Best
Sir Olivers Song
Spirit of Praise 1 & 2
The Birthday Party
The Gift of Praise
The Glory of Christmas
The Maranatha! Songbook
The New Redemption Hymnal
The Rainbow Songbook
The Victor
The Witness

Appendix 6
Signatories to the Berne and Universal Copyright Conventions ___

The following list of 105 countries who are signatories of either or both of the major international copyright conventions is believed to be correct as at 1 March 1989.

The Secretariat of the Berne Convention (81 countries) is operated by the World Intellectual Property Organization (WIPO) in Geneva. The Secretariat of the Universal Copyright Convention (81 countries) is the responsibility of UNESCO in Paris. Their addresses are given in Appendix 2.

	Berne	Universal		Berne	Universal
Algeria		U	Chile	B	U
Andorra		U	Colombia	B	U
Argentina	B	U	Congo	B	
Australia	B	U	Costa Rica	B	U
Austria	B	U	Cuba		U
Bahamas	B	U	Cyprus	B	
Bangladesh		U	Czechoslovakia	B	U
Barbados	B	U	Denmark	B	U
Belguim	B	U	Dominican		
Belize		U	Republic		U
Benin	B		Ecuador		U
Brazil	B	U	Egypt	B	
Bulgaria	B	U	El Salvador		U
Burkina Faso	B		Fiji	B	U
Cameroon	B	U	Finland	B	U
Canada	B	U	France	B	U
Central African			Gabon	B	
Republic	B		German Demo-		
Chad	B		cratic Republic	B	U

	Berne	Universal		Berne	Universal
Germany (Federal Republic)	B	U	Nigeria		U
			Norway	B	U
Ghana		U	Pakistan	B	U
Greece	B	U	Panama		U
Guatemala		U	Paraguay		U
Guinea	B	U	Peru	B	U
Haiti		U	Philippines	B	U
Hungary	B	U	Poland	B	U
Iceland	B	U	Portugal	B	U
India	B	U	Roumania	B	
Ireland	B	U	Rwanda	B	
Israel	B	U	Saint Vincent		
Italy	B	U	and the		
Ivory Coast	B		Grenadines		U
Japan	B	U	Senegal	B	U
Kampuchea			South Africa	B	
(Democratic)		U	Soviet Union		U
Kenya		U	Spain	B	U
Korea (Republic)		U	Sri Lanka	B	U
Laos		U	Surinam	B	
Lebanon	B	U	Sweden	B	U
Liberia	B	U	Switzerland	B	U
Libya	B		Thailand	B	
Liechtenstein	B	U	Togo	B	
Luxembourg	B	U	Trinidad and		
Madagascar	B		Tobago	B	U
Malawi		U	Tunisia	B	U
Mali	B		Turkey	B	
Malta	B	U	United Kingdom	B	U
Mauritania	B		United States of		
Mauritius		U	America	B	U
Mexico	B	U	Uruguay	B	
Monaco	B	U	Vatican	B	U
Morocco	B	U	Venezuela	B	U
Netherlands	B	U	Yugoslavia	B	U
New Zealand	B	U	Zaire	B	
Nicaragua		U	Zambia		U
Niger	B		Zimbabwe	B	

Appendix 7
Further reading _____

Various publications available in the United Kingdom were prepared prior to the introduction of the Copyright, Designs and Patents Act 1988. These are intentionally not listed in view of the fact that they are primarily based upon the Copyright Act 1956, which has been replaced by the 1988 Act.

Channel Four TV Programme Recording (Guild Learning)

Clarion (Copyright Licensing Agency)

Code of Fair Practice agreed between composers, publishers and users of printed music (Music Publishers' Association)

Copyright, Designs and Patents Act 1988 (HMSO)

Green Paper on Copyright and the Challenge of Technology 1988 (Commission of the European Communities)

International Publishers' Bulletin (IPA)

Mechanical Copyright series (MCPS)

A Question of Copyright, second edition (Jay books)

The Use of Video Recorders in Schools (IBA)

Worship Magazine (Christian Music Association)

Index ─────────────────────────────────